Table Talk

Table Talk

Beginning the Sunday Conversation on the Gospel of Luke (Year C)

Jay Cormier

New City Press
Hyde Park, New York

For Father Robert Biron

Published in the United States by New City Press
202 Cardinal Rd., Hyde Park, NY 12538
www.newcitypress.com

Cover design by Durva Correia

Library of Congress Cataloging-in-Publication Data:

Cormier, Jay.
Table talk : beginning the conversation on the Gospel of Luke / Jay Cormier.
p. cm.
Includes bibliographical references.
ISBN 978-1-56548-322-4 (year C : pbk. : alk. paper) 1. Bible. N.T. Luke—Meditations.
2. Church year meditations. 3. Common lectionary (1992) I. Title.
BS2595.54.C67 2009
242′.3—dc22
2009021054

Printed in the United States of America

Contents

Advent

Christmas

Lent

The Easter Triduum

Easter

Solemnities of the Lord in Ordinary Time

Ordinary Time

Introduction

This book is designed to begin a *conversation,* a conversation that takes place each Sunday at the table of the Lord.

The conversation begins with a particular memory of the extraordinary life of the Gospel Jesus: a story he told, a wonder he worked; a confrontation with the establishment, a misunderstanding with his disciples; remembering when he cried, when he despaired, when he was abandoned, when he got angry; the injustice of his condemnation, the horror of his death, the vindication of his resurrection.

The conversation then seeks to understand what this memory of Jesus means to us in the marketplaces and temples of our time and place. In word and sacrament, we share the wonders of healing and forgiveness that Jesus is performing in our midst.

It's a conversation that shows no signs of being exhausted.

It is the writer's hope that these pages will provoke *Table Talk* — reflection and insight about God's Word as it is proclaimed at the table of the Lord on Sunday. The focus here is on the Sunday Gospel — the climactic reading at the Sunday Eucharist in which God speaks to us, touches us, loves us in the story of Jesus, God's Christ, *Emmanuel.*

The reflections offered here are one poor pilgrim's attempt to grasp the Gospel after many journeys through the lectionary as a writer, teacher and struggling disciple. These essays are intended to help spark the Sunday conversation around your parish table: to be starting points for the homilist who will preach on the Gospel, the catechist who will teach that Gospel to children, the RCIA team who will lead candidates through a discussion of the passage, or the individual disciple looking for a companion on his/her day-to-day journey to Emmaus.

(This volume follows the pericopes of both the Roman Catholic lectionary and the common lectionary used by many Protestant churches. Where different Gospel readings are assigned, reflections on each reading are offered).

The problem with a collection like this is that it might be perceived as a final word, a definitive reading, a complete analysis of the Sunday Gospel reading. This book is no such thing. It is one "converser's" reflection and best reading of these Gospel stories after many years of his own prayer, reflection and teaching. Perhaps you will find here few nuggets of gold from a very deep mine; more gifted and wiser miners will find much more of value as they dig deeper and deeper.

If this book helps you begin that conversation at your own table this Sunday or helps you in your own search and study, these pages will have done their job.

Advent

First Sunday of Advent

"When you see these signs begin to happen, stand erect and raise your heads because your redemption is at hand."

Luke 21: 25–28, 34–36

The sign of the diaper and car seat

For the umpteenth time, you're changing your baby's diaper; or you're unbuckling your child from the car seat and lifting him out and then repeating the process in reverse later. You're exhausted. Granted, these are not moments usually given to great spiritual insight. But as you fasten the diaper, your little girl giggles; as you struggle to maneuver the safety seat, your little boy gives you a hug. And in that moment, you are filled with the incredible joy and wonder of this miracle before you.

Or you are balancing your checkbook or completing your tax return. Making the dollars stretch to cover all the family expenses can be a delicate balancing act. But our checkbooks and tax returns are unmistakable signs of how lucky and blessed we are. While we're not quite on the Fortune 500 list, most of us have built comfortable lives for ourselves and our families. And that's reason enough for gratitude.

Or you and your spouse are doing errands at the mall. As you have done since you dated, you hold hands. And it dawns on you how happy you are to be married to this person, how your love has remained constant through births and deaths and triumphs and disappointments and diapers and report cards and mortgages and errands at the mall.

On this First Sunday of Advent, Jesus calls us to pay attention, to wake up and realize the many "signs" of God's love in our midst. In the middle of our own individual disasters and calamities, God somehow manages to make his healing and compassionate presence known — if we are attentive enough to realize it.

Advent begins at the end — the promised return of Christ at the end of time. For the faithful disciple, history is a moving forward, a journey to the fulfillment of God's reign when God's Christ will return as Lord of all. We therefore live in a permanent state of Advent: the disciple's life is one of watchfulness, preparation and perseverance as we await the return of the Holy One. Jesus calls us to pay attention to the "signs" of God's Advent presence, to "stand erect and raise our heads," to realize God's presence in our midst.

The moments we are given in this experience of life are precious and few. God gives us these days in order that we might come to discover him and know him in the love of others and the goodness of this world in anticipation of the next.

Come, Lord, into the Advent of our lives.
Open our eyes and hearts to recognize the signs
of your love in our midst
that every moment of life you have given us
may be lived in the peace that is possible
only in humble gratitude and joyful selflessness.

Second Sunday of Advent

John went throughout the whole region of the Jordan, proclaiming a baptism of repentance for the forgiveness of sins.

Luke 3: 1–6

The prophet at the galleria

He caused quite a commotion among the holiday shoppers. Dressed in a tattered flannel shirt and jeans, he was sometimes spotted rummaging around the dumpsters for scraps from the food vendors. No one knew where he spent his nights. Despite his ragged appearance and that slightly "off" look in his eyes, there was a kindness and sincerity about him that attracted people to him.

He would station himself by one of the fountains in the galleria and stop shoppers. He would ask them why they would spend so much money for Christmas, why they would allow themselves to become so obsessed and stressed over this tinseled holiday.

We like our Christmas with a lot of sugar, don't we? he would tease. *Christmas is about hope and love — and that can be a struggle. Give gifts of kindness and compassion to another. Seek forgiveness and reconciliation from family and friends who are lost. Let the spirit of the Christ Child embrace every season of the year.*

Everyone who listened to him would nod in agreement — as they nervously tightened their grips on their shopping bags. Some were moved to quit shopping and go home to be with their families, others would go off and buy an extra toy or piece of clothing for charity; a few would even escape to a church or chapel for quiet prayer.

Sometimes he would rail against the insipid music and the gaudy decorations. When the mall Santa would walk by, he would make fun of him, asking the embarrassed Santa pointed questions about the real Christmas story.

Soon, though, the storeowners had had enough of his distractions. The mall managers had security escort him from the premises.

He wasn't really hurting anyone, they realized.

But he had to go, they said.
He was ruining everyone's Christmas.

If John the Baptizer appeared in our time and place, this is where he might be found, how he would probably look, what he would undoubtedly say. On this Second Sunday of Advent, John makes his annual appearance — intrusion? — into our Advent busyness. So important is the emergence of John the Baptizer in the Christ event that Luke dates his appearance six different ways. In his Gospel, Luke introduces John as prophets were introduced in the First Testament ("the word of God was spoken to John son of Zechariah in the desert"). As does Matthew and Mark, Luke cites the famous passage from Isaiah prophesying "a herald's voice in the desert" to describe the Baptizer's mission — but Luke quotes more of the Isaiah prophecy than his synoptic counterparts, including the promise of universal salvation that is so central to Luke's Gospel.

Forms of "baptism" were common in the Judaism of Gospel times — in some Jewish communities, it was through baptism rather than circumcision that a Gentile became a Jew. But John's baptism was distinctive. His baptism at the Jordan was a rite of repentance and metanoia — a conversion of heart and spirit. The Baptizer's ministry fulfilled the promise of Ezekiel (Ezekiel 36: 25–26): that, at the dawn of a new age, the God of Israel would purify his people from their sins with clean water and instill in them a new heart and spirit.

John, the Advent prophet, proclaims the real Christmas event: the coming of the Christ — God becoming one of us out of love for us. The Baptizer calls us to joyful hope in God's constant presence among us, a presence that we are often too busy or too jaded or too overwhelmed to realize. But the notion of "joy to the world" and "peace on earth to all people of good will" that we give at least a hearing to this time of year can be just as real and life-giving in every season of the year: in imitating the loving kindness, the compassionate forgiveness and the reconciling selflessness of Jesus we make God's living presence a reality in every human heart, in every moment of time, in every gathering place.

The same Word that came to John in the desert comes to each of us in the deserts of our own hearts, enabling us to transform the wastelands and straighten the winding roads of our lives in the compassion and justice of God. Each one of us is called to be a *prophet* of Christ — to "proclaim" (the Greek word for *prophet),* in our ministries, in our compassion and generosity, in our courageous and constant commitment to what is right that Jesus the Messiah has come.

Gracious God,
make us prophets of your Son's coming into our midst;
make us disciples of the Messiah's Word
  of justice and peace;
make us "Christ-bearers" of your forgiveness
  and compassion
to all your sons and daughters.

Third Sunday of Advent

"Whoever has two cloaks should give to the one who has none ... Stop collecting more than what is prescribed ... Do not practice extortion, do not falsely accuse anyone, and be satisfied with your wages."

Luke 3: 10–18

A case of accidental Christmas cheer

A true story, recounted in the delightful "Metropolitan Diary" column of *The New York Times*:

Rather than cash in her cans and bottles, she either tosses her bag of empties into the nearest trash can or hands it over to one of the street people in the neighborhood.

Two days before Christmas, she was off to exchange a Christmas gift at Eddie Bauer, carrying her bag of empties to give away. The first street person she encountered was not one of the neighborhood regulars but she handed him the bag anyway, saying that she would probably have lots more for him on Sunday after her dinner party. The fellow stared at the bag, then at her, and then said goodbye.

She then continued on her way. She had taken a few steps when she heard the clinking of empty metal cans in the bag she was carrying. She immediately realized that she had given him the Eddie Bauer bag with the man's turtleneck pullover, size large. She headed back to where she had last seen him but he was nowhere in sight.

She saw him again the following night. It was Christmas Eve and he was stooped over a trash can collecting bottles. "Remember me?" she asked. "I gave you a shopping bag yesterday."

"Yes," he said. "I also have new pants, and tomorrow I'm wearing them with the sweater. Thanks." And he went back to sorting.

She knows exactly what she'll do in Christmases to come. And she'll gift wrap.[1]

This woman's newfound Christmas spirit mirrors the Baptizer's preaching in today's Gospel.

The Baptizer is approached by two groups whose professions were scorned by the Pharisees: tax collectors, who usually made handsome profits by gouging their fellow Jews, and Jewish soldiers who belonged to the Roman peacekeeping force. John requires of them not a change of professions but a change of heart and attitude, that they perform their duties with honesty and integrity. John calls for selfless concern for one's disadvantaged brothers and sisters.

John assures his Jewish listeners that he is not the Messiah; in fact, John considers himself lower than the lowest slaves (only a non-Jewish slave could be required to loosen his master's sandal strap and John does not presume to do even that).

John is clear that his role is that of messenger for the One who is to come — a role that now belongs to each one of us of this second Advent who have been baptized in the Spirit of the Christ.

In proclaiming the Messiah's "baptism in the Holy Spirit and fire," John employs the image of a "winnowing-fan." A winnowing-fan was a flat, wooden, shovel-like tool, used to toss grain into the air. The heavier grain fell to the ground and the chaff blew away. In the same way, John says, the Messiah will come to gather the "remnant" of Israel and destroy the Godless.

Through baptism, we take on the role of loving servant imitating Christ whose name we claim. As John preaches at the Jordan, we are called to be witnesses of God's love by the love we extend to others; prophets of his justice by our unfailing commitment to what is right and good; lamps reflecting the light of God's Christ in our forgiveness, mercy and compassion; harvesters of souls through our humble and dedicated servanthood.

Come, Lord, and gather us together as your holy people.
As you have baptized us with water,
send your Spirit upon us to do the work of baptism:
to be prophets of justice
and ministers of compassion
along the Jordans and in the Nazareths and Jersualems
of our own time and place.

Fourth Sunday of Advent

When Elizabeth heard Mary's greeting, the infant leaped in her womb and Elizabeth, filled with the Holy Spirit, cried out in a loud voice and said, "Blessed are you among women, and blessed is the fruit of your womb …"

Luke 1: 39–45

A pregnant season

After a long, tiring trip, the young woman arrives at the home of her cousin, who is several years older. She has come to care for her cousin, who has found herself expecting a child, despite her advanced age.

The young woman is also pregnant. Her excitement over motherhood is mixed with fear and anxiety; but her cousin's joy at this unexpected grace knows no end.

For both mothers-to-be, it is a time of vulnerability. Every action, every decision is made in light of the child: *Is it safe for me to do this? Will it harm my child if I eat that?* On the one hand, the expectant mother feels as if she is walking on eggshells; on the other, she has all the mobility of a whale.

For both mothers-to-be, pregnancy is a time of waiting, of sacrifice, of anxiety. When it is over, they will remember their nine-month "confinements" as nothing, their painful labor hardly worth talking about. Every loss fades into the light of this gain, this precious and irreplaceable child.

For both mothers-to-be, life's center has shifted. The old controls, successes and defenses don't matter so much. The child changes all of that.

For both mothers-to-be, God has touched their lives in the child within them.

The readings for the Fourth Sunday of Advent each year shift the focus from Advent's call to preparation for the Messiah to setting the stage for the Christmas event. In today's Gospel, Elizabeth proclaims her joy-filled faith in God's promise of salvation that will be accomplished through Mary's child and praises her young cousin for her "yes" to God's plan.

The meeting of Mary and Elizabeth in today's Gospel is a beautiful portrait of the meaning of this Advent season. Their pending motherhood echoes Advent's invitation to embrace the joy and fulfillment that can only be found beyond ourselves and in finding God in others; of life as a blessed time to be lived in the search for the holy and sacred in our midst; of understanding that suffering and pain and hard work are the only paths to building a life worth living; of the never-disappointing hope that is found only in the things of God; that God is present to us and calling us to him regardless of fears, doubts and poor sense of self-esteem and worthiness. May we experience the joy, hope and excitement of Mary and Elizabeth in their Visitation within our own lives and families in every season of every year.

God of all times and ages,
come and make your dwelling place in our midst.
May your love be our house of safety, of consolation;
may your peace be the table where we gather;
may your forgiveness be the hearth that warms us
and brings us together.

Christmas

Christmas: The Nativity of the Lord

"Silent night ..."

Silent night, holy night, / All is calm, all is bright ...

A holy night, to be sure. But neither "silent" nor "calm."

That night in Bethlehem was anything but Christmas-card serene. In a cold dark cave used as a barn, a frightened young woman gave birth to her child, amid the cries and howls, the bleating and the braying. Finally, a newborn's first cries for life broke the stillness. This "silent night" was filled with fear, pain and exhaustion of childbirth that sleep alone does not relieve.

There was no "calm" that night in crowded, chaotic Bethlehem, a little hamlet bursting at the seams with visitors and travelers who had come for the great census. There was no "calm" in all of Israel — only tension and conflict between the Jewish people and their Roman occupiers. Palestine of the first-century was hardly a place of "heavenly peace" — it was a land torn apart by oppression, persecution, and terror.

"Silent night?" Listen again.

"All is bright?" The darkness of fear and chaos reigned.

"All is calm?" Not that night. Not there.

And yet on this noisy, chaotic, anxious night, Christ was born. Sheltered in a dark cave, the light of Christ dawned. Amid the pain and anguish of a broken people, Christ came with new hope and transforming joy.

In the middle of our own dark nights of pain and anguish, God comes and transforms them into "holy" nights of his peace. Amid the noise and clamor that consume us, the voice of God speaks to us in the "silence" of our hearts. This Christmas night, the compassion of God transforms all of our nights and days in the "brightness" of "heavenly peace."

The lectionary provides four pericopes recounting the events of this "silent night/holy night":

Mass of the Vigil

"Joseph, son of David, do not be afraid to take Mary your wife into your home. For it is through the Holy Spirit that this child has been conceived in her."

Matthew 1: 1–25 [18–25]

For Matthew, the story of Jesus begins with the promise to Abraham — that Jesus is the ultimate and perfect fulfillment of the Law and Prophets. So Matthew begins his Gospel with "a family record" of Jesus, tracing the infant's birth from Abraham (highlighting his Jewish identity) and David (his Messiahship). The accuracy of Matthew's list is dubious; but presenting an historic record is not the evangelist's point. Matthew proclaims in his genealogy that this Jesus is the fulfillment of a world that God envisioned from the first moment of creation — a world created in the justice and peace that is the very nature of its Creator.

Matthew's version of Jesus' birth at Bethlehem follows. This is not Luke's familiar story of a child born in a Bethlehem stable and greeted by shepherds and angels, but that of a young unmarried woman suddenly finding herself pregnant and her very hurt and confused husband wondering what to do. In Gospel times, marriage was agreed upon by the groom and the bride's parents almost immediately after the age of puberty; but the girl continued to live with her parents after the wedding until the husband was able to support her in his home or that of his parents. During that interim period, marital intercourse was not permitted. Yet Mary is found to be with child.

Joseph, an observant but compassionate Jew, does not wish to subject Mary to the full fury of Jewish law, so he plans to divorce her "quietly." But in images reminiscent of the Old Testament "annunciations" of Isaac and Samuel, an angel appears to Joseph in a dream and reveals that this child is the fulfillment of Isaiah's prophecy. Because of his complete faith and trust in God's promise, Joseph acknowledges the child and names him *Jesus* ("Savior") and becomes, in the eyes of the Law, the legal father of Jesus. Thus, Jesus, through Joseph, is born a descendent of David.

The theme of Matthew's infancy narrative is *Emmanuel* — that Jesus is the promised Christ of old. Isaiah's prophecy has finally been fulfilled in Jesus: the virgin has given birth to a son, one who is a descendent of David's house (through Joseph). Jesus is truly *Emmanuel* — "God is with us."

Mass at Midnight

"For today in the city of David a savior has been born to you who is Christ and Lord."

Luke 2: 1–14

Centuries of hope in God's promise have come to fulfillment: the Messiah is born!

Luke's account of Jesus' birth begins by placing the event during the reign of Caesar Augustus. Augustus, who ruled from 27 BC until 14 AD, was honored as "savior" and "god" in ancient Greek inscriptions. His long reign was hailed as the pax Augusta — a period of peace throughout the vast Roman world. Luke deliberately points out that it is during the rule of Augustus — the savior, god and peace-maker — that Jesus the Christ, the long-awaited Savior and Messiah, the Son of God and Prince of Peace, enters human history.

Throughout Luke's Gospel, it is the poor, the lowly, the outcast and the rejected who immediately embrace the preaching of Jesus. The announcement of the Messiah's birth to shepherds — who were among the most isolated and despised in the Jewish community — reflects Luke's theme that the poor are the blessed of God.

Mass at Dawn

"Let us go, then, to Bethlehem to see this thing that has taken place which the Lord has made known to us."

Luke 2: 15–20

Typical of Luke's Gospel, it is the shepherds of Bethlehem — among the poorest and most disregarded of Jewish society — who become the first messengers of the Gospel.

From the Christmas story in Luke's Gospel, we have a romantic image of shepherds as gentle, peaceful figures. But the manger scene image is a far cry from the reality: The shepherds of Biblical times were tough, earthy characters who fearlessly used their clubs to defend their flocks from wolves and other wild animals. They had even less patience for the pompous scribes and Pharisees who treated them as second- and third-class citizens, barring these ill-bred rustics from the synagogue and courts.

Yet it was to shepherds that God first revealed the birth of the Messiah. The shepherds' vision on the Bethlehem hillside proclaims to all people of every place and generation that Christ comes for the sake of all of humankind.

Luke adds this touching detail: "Mary kept all these things, reflecting on them in her heart." As every parent remembers the birth of their son or daughter, Mary would relive these remarkable events, seeking to grasp the extraordinary love of God in this life she has brought into the world. With Mary, we remember the promise of this holy night when God touches human history; with Mary, we struggle to understand how this night transforms all of our days; with Mary, we seek to live the story of Christ in the joys and sorrows of our own stories.

Mass of the Day

And the Word became flesh and made his dwelling among us ...

John 1: 1–18

The Gospel for Christmas Day is the beautiful Prologue hymn to John's Gospel. With echoes of Genesis 1 ("In the beginning ..." "the light shines on in darkness ... "), the Prologue exalts Christ as the creative Word of God that comes as the new light to illuminate God's re-creation.

In the original Greek text, the phrase "made his dwelling place among us" is more literally translated as "pitched his tent or tabernacle." The image evokes the Exodus memory of the tent pitched by Israelites for the Ark of the Covenant. God sets up the tabernacle of the new covenant in the body of the Child of Bethlehem.

The reading from John reminds us that Christmas is more than the birth of a child; it is the beginning of the Christ event that will transform and re-create human history, a presence that continues to this day and for all time. In this child, the extraordinary love of God has taken our "flesh" and "made his dwelling among us." In his "Word made flesh," God touches us at the very core of our being, perfectly expressing his constant and unchanging love.

Lord God,
with wonder and gratitude we behold the birth
 of your Christ.
May his birth illuminate our dark nights
 with the brightness of your love;
may the good news we hear
 in our own chaotic and struggling Bethlehems
 bring joy and hope to all our mornings;
may the poverty of his birth and life among us help us
 to recognize our own poverty;
may his coming to us as one of us inspire us
 to lift up one another in the dignity of being
 your sons and daughters.

After three days, they found Jesus in the temple, sitting in the midst of the teachers, listening to them and asking them questions, and all who heard him were astounded at his understanding and his answers. "Why were you looking for me? Did you not know that I must be in my Father's house?"

Luke 2: 41–52
[Roman lectionary]

In the country of fear

It is a journey we all make at some time in our lives, sometimes more than once. We make the trek accompanied by family and friends — or we travel alone. We never forget our travels in the country of fear.

Fear — that place far away from home, a place so foreign to us.

Fear — a country of unfamiliar typography and tongues, an ocean of strangers, where we are assailed by the unknown, where we stumble, reeling from distress and grief.

Fear — a mysterious place of unimaginable and astonishing wonders.

In the country of fear, you are never physically comfortable; you never relax or sleep. In the country of fear, you are gripped in grogginess, illness, depression, despair. In the country of fear, it is difficult to hear what another says, it is a struggle to grasp reality.

The soul facing death and the helpless family by his or her side walks the dark road through the country of fear.

The abandoned spouse can suddenly find himself or herself hopelessly lost in the country of fear.

The parents searching for their lost child desperately struggle through the country of fear.

Yet it is in the country of fear where we find our true selves.

It is through the country of fear that we find our way home.

And the only path through the country of fear is love; the only light is compassion.[1]

The family of Jesus, Mary and Joseph knew all too well the country of fear. Like families of every time and place, they experienced hardship and pain: they faced a difficult and unexpected pregnancy; they were forced from their home because of the tyrant Herod; and in today's Gospel, they experience every parents' worst nightmare: the disappearance of their child. But they make their way through the country of fear by the love that binds them together as a couple and as a family, the love that makes their poor home a place of welcome and acceptance, a harbor of forgiveness and compassion. It is that love that is celebrated in today's liturgy.

The story of Mary and Joseph's three days of anguish as they searched for their child was probably a later addition to Luke's Gospel, originating in the rich oral tradition of stories told about Jesus. Like many childhood stories of famous people, this story had been told again and again because it showed signs in Jesus' boyhood of the qualities that will emerge in his adulthood marking his life forever in history. Luke clearly has the events of Holy Week in mind in the details he has included in the story: the journey to Jerusalem at Passover, the encounter with the teachers at the Temple, the three days Jesus is lost.

At the age of 12, a Jewish boy becomes a "son of the Law" — he becomes personally responsible for following the Torah. The faithful Jesus reveals himself as the perfect servant of his Father from the time of his first legal pilgrimage to Jerusalem.

In Gospel times, teachers of the Torah conducted classes not in a lecture format but as an open discussion in which participants were encouraged to ask questions. To suggest, as some old paintings depict, that Jesus dominated the scene, overwhelming the teachers with the depth of his insights, is inaccurate. As Luke tells the story, Jesus was listening to the teachers and eagerly searching for knowledge in his questions like a highly motivated and interested student typically much older than the 12-year-old boy from Nazareth.

Luke concludes his chapter on Jesus' birth and childhood by noting that Mary "kept all these things in her heart." Perhaps

Mary confronted for the first time the reality that this would not be her last journey through the country of fear.

Loving Father,
keep our family within the embrace
  of your loving providence.
In times of crisis and tension,
bless our families with the hope of your consolation
  and forgiveness;
in times of joy and growth,
bless us with a spirit of thankfulness,
never let us forget that you are Father of us all,
the Giver of all that is good.

Sunday after Christmas

In the beginning was the Word, and the Word was with God, and the Word was God … And the Word became flesh and lived among us, and we have seen his glory, the glory of a father's only son, full of grace and truth.

John 1: 1–18
[Common lectionary — NRSV]

The Luck of Roaring Camp

In his volumes of short stories, Bret Hart depicted the rough and gritty characters of the American Wild West of the 18th century.

In one of his stories, "The Luck of Roaring Camp," a pregnant, sick Indian woman stumbles into a camp of gruff, hard-drinking, fierce prospectors. Two of the men suddenly find themselves in the alien world of midwifery. Although the mother dies, her child, a boy, survives.

Deaths were pretty common in Roaring Camp, but a birth was something entirely new. Immediately, the men of Roaring Camp assume responsibility for the boy. They take turns caring for him. They build a cabin, not a makeshift shack, but "clean, boarded and papered" — complete with lace curtains! As they care for the boy, they begin to shed their roughness and cool their tempers. They begin to see the community and world as much bigger than their own dreams of gold. To hold the child or sing to him was considered a privilege. They demand from one another such previously unheard-of things in Roaring Camp as cleanliness, quiet and civility. They come to consider the child not a burden but a gift — and name him "Luck," Thomas Luck.

Little Thomas Luck transformed this outpost of rough, crude miners into a community of generosity, tenderness and compassion. The child brought forth from these reckless characters and criminals dignity, humility and a sense of beauty, wonder and joy. An old frontier expression took on new meaning for Roaring Camp: "The luck was with them."

Christ has come — the very Word and Light of God dwells in our midst. In his birth, we are reborn; in his humanity, our humanity is made sacred; in his life, God touches all of human history with compassion, joy and peace.

At Christmas, the sacred is no longer some abstract concept of theological theory; God has descended from the heavens to become one of us in order to show us how we might become like him. The love of God takes on a human face, the Word of God becomes "enfleshed" in the Christ child, enabling us to transform our hearts in that love and re-create our world in that Word of justice and compassion. This child is the very light of God, who inspires hearts and spirits to welcome children as gifts of God, to find joy and completeness in loving our beloved, to care for the poorest and neediest creature as if he or she is Christ himself.

Christmas invites us to embrace the wondrous mystery and the transforming reality of this birth in the quiet of our hearts and the everyday peace of our homes.

Christ Jesus, you are the Word that set all of creation
  into motion;
you are the Light that illuminates every human life;
you are the love of God in flesh and blood.
Let your Word echo in our hearts that we
  may re-create the world in the Father's compassion;
let your light shatter the darkness of sin and alienation;
let your love be the glory we seek,
  as we struggle to imitate
your example of humble and grateful service
  to one another.

January 1

Mary, the Mother of God
[Roman lectionary]

The Holy Name of Jesus
[Common lectionary]

When eight days were completed for his circumcision, he was named Jesus …

Luke 2: 16–21

"To give birth to God"

The great Dominican theologian Meister Eckhart preached that "we are all meant to be mothers of God" for "God is always waiting to be born."

God is waiting to be born in our own loveless stables and forgotten caves. God is waiting to be born in the Bethlehems of anger, estrangement and hopelessness. God is waiting to be born in the Nazareths of our own homes, schools and workplaces.

On this New Year's Day, the lectionary recalls the liturgical and legal marking of Jesus' birth. Eight days after he is born in Bethlehem, Jesus becomes a member of the Jewish nation by the ancient rite of circumcision. Mary and Joseph's child is given the name *Yeshua* — "The Lord saves." The rite of circumcision unites Mary's child with the chosen people and makes him an heir to the promises God made to Abraham — promises to be fulfilled in the Child himself.

In the Roman Catholic tradition, today's solemnity honors Mary under her most ancient title — Theotokos, "Bearer of God": In accepting her role as mother of the Messiah, she becomes the first disciple of her Son, the first to embrace his Gospel of hope, compassion and reconciliation. As Mary, the young unmarried pregnant girl, believes and trusts in the incredible thing that she is to be a part of (who "kept all these things, reflecting on them in her heart"), even the most ordinary of us can believe in our parts in the drama, too.

In other traditions, January 1 honors the Holy Name of Jesus. Today's liturgy centers on the Gospel account of Jesus' circumcision at which he is given the name that not only identifies him but also marks the life he will live for the sake of humanity. It is the name we take on in our baptismal commitment to live the life of his Gospel. By his name, we are called to "give birth" to God in the stables and barns of our own time and place. "The Lord saves" in every work of compassion and mercy we extend, in the peace and justice we struggle to bring to our own Bethlehems and Nazareths and Jerusalems.

Father of compassion,
in baptism we have taken on the name of your Son:
    Jesus, "The Lord saves";
    Christ, "the anointed of God."
May we live that name every day of this new New Year:
may we create a dwelling place for you
in our works of charity and reconciliation;
may we give birth to you
in every word of consolation and support we speak,
in every joy we bring into the lives of others.

Epiphany

Magi from the east arrived in Jerusalem; "Where is the newborn king of the Jews? We saw his star at its rising and have come to do him homage."

Matthew 2: 1–12

"Journey of the Magi"

A cold coming we had of it.
Just the worst time of the year
For a journey, and such a long journey:
The ways deep and the weather sharp,
The very dead of winter.

So begins T.S. Eliot's beautiful poem "Journey of the Magi."

The poem's narrator is one of the travelers we read about in today's Gospel. He remembers their difficult adventure many years before: the cold nights spent on the frozen wasteland, the stubbornness of the sore-footed camels, the hostile and unwelcoming cities along the way. More than once they wondered if their search for the king-priest was folly.

Finally, the narrator remembers, they came to a warm valley, with running streams and trees and vegetation. After many inquiries, they arrived at the place they were looking for. So extraordinary was this Child that all he can say about the memory is: *Finding the place, it was (you may say) satisfactory.*

The traveler, now an old man, says that he would do it all again — but he still wonders:

... were we led all that way for Birth or Death?
There was a Birth, certainly,
We had evidence and no doubt.
I had seen birth and death,

But had thought they were different;
this Birth was hard and bitter agony for us,
like Death, our death.
We returned to our places, these Kingdoms,
But no longer at ease here …
I should be glad of another death.

The story of the magi's search for the newborn Christ is not a romantic tale with a happy ending. It is the beginning of a story of suffering and hardship and death; it is the prelude to a lifelong struggle to bring justice to a place broken by conflict, to heal a people scarred by war and hatred. Yet the Gospel of God's Christ is a story of hope amid the bloodshed, of life conquering death, of love rising from the ashes.

The story of the astrologers and the star of Bethlehem is unique to Matthew's Gospel. Note that Matthew does not call them kings nor does he give their names nor reports where they came from — in fact, Matthew never even specifies the number of magi (because three gifts are presented to the Child, it has been a tradition since the fifth century to picture "three wise men"). In stripping away the romantic layers that have been added to the story over the centuries, Matthew's point becomes clearer.

A great many Old Testament ideas and images are presented in this story of *epiphany* (from the Greek word for *appearance* or *manifestation).* The star, for example, is reminiscent of Balaam's prophecy that "a star shall advance from Jacob" (Numbers 24:17). Many of the details in Matthew's story about the child Jesus parallel the story of the child Moses and the Exodus.

Most importantly, Matthew's story provides a preview of what is to come. First, the reactions of the various parties to the birth of Jesus mirror the effects Jesus' teaching will have on those who hear it. Herod reacts with anger and hostility to the Jesus of the poor who comes to overturn the powerful and rich. The chief priest and scribes greet with haughty indifference the news of a Jesus who comes to give new life and meaning to their cherished rituals and laws. But the magi — non-believers in the eyes of Israel — possess the humility of faith and the openness of mind and heart to seek and welcome the Jesus who will institute the Second Covenant between God and the New Israel.

The gifts of the astrologers indicate the principal dimensions of Jesus' mission:

- **gold** is a gift fitting for a king, a ruler, one with power and authority;
- **frankincense** is a gift fitting for a priest, one who offers sacrifice (frankincense was an aromatic perfume sprinkled on the animals sacrificed in the Temple);
- **myrrh** is a fitting "gift" for someone who is to die (myrrh was used in ancient times for embalming the bodies of the dead before burial).

The traveler in T.S. Eliot's poem and his companions have encountered Christ — and their lives have been changed forever: It is, as the old traveler remembers, a death to his own self-absorption and a birth to something greater than himself. May our encounter with Christ — in the Sunday Gospels of this new year, in our everyday lives of both struggle and grace — be a constant epiphany of re-creating and transforming our lives in the love of *Emmanuel* — "God with us."

Christ, the very light of God,
be the star we follow on our journey
to the dwelling place of God;
in your light, may we recognize all men and women
as our brothers and sisters under the loving providence
of the Father of all.
Illuminate the roads and paths we travel,
that we may not stumble or turn back
from your way of peace, forgiveness and justice.

After Jesus was baptized, heaven opened and the Holy Spirit descended upon him in bodily form like a dove. And a voice came from heaven, "You are my beloved Son; with you I am well pleased."

Luke 3: 15–16, 21–22

"Namaste"

David Whyte's poem "The Old Interior Angel" (from his book *Fire in the Earth)* is the story of a young American traveler hiking in the mountains of Tibet and Nepal. The young man came to a broken footbridge, hundreds of feet over a rocky stream. The cables had snapped and the wooden planks tumbled together uselessly. Clearly, he could go no further. The strong and usually confident young man could not bring himself to cross the trembling, ruined bridge. Admitting defeat, he decided to turn back.

As he was about to leave, an old woman, bent and barefoot, with an enormous basket balanced on her back, approached. She had been collecting dung for fuel along the path. Seeing the young man, she smiled and extended the traditional greeting, "*Namaste*" — "I greet the God in you."

The young man bowed in response, but before he could look up again, the old woman was gone, having almost floated straight across the treacherous broken bridge that seemed to him so impassable.

Without thinking, swept up in the wake of her courage and trust, he prayed *Namaste* and followed.

Namaste — "I greet the God in you."

What the people of Himalayas call *Namaste* mirrors the Spirit that descends upon Jesus as he comes up from the waters of Jordan. The Spirit, *Namaste*, speaks to every human being in the deepest and most hidden part of our hearts about the love and compassion of God; it is the very life of God animating us and leading us; it is a wellspring of grace and wisdom, of courage and perseverance, enabling us to make our way over the rugged mountain paths and treacherous bridges of every life's journey.

Today's Gospel is the final event of Christ's Epiphany: Jesus' baptism at the Jordan River by John. Our Christmas celebration officially comes to an end today at the banks of the Jordan. Jesus is no longer the child of the Bethlehem manger but the adult Redeemer making his way to Jerusalem. The good news spoken by the angels continues to unfold; the most wondrous part of the Christ story is yet to be revealed.

So important was his baptism to the early Church's understanding of Jesus that all four evangelists record the event. Luke presents Jesus as the last person to be baptized by John, bringing John's ministry to completion.

Luke's account of the scene employs many images from the Old Testament:

- the sky opens ("Oh, that you would rend the heavens and come down" — Isaiah 63: 19);
- the Spirit "descended upon him like a dove" (many rabbis likened the wind above the waters at the dawn of Genesis to a dove hovering above its newborn; in employing this image, Luke suggests that, in this Jesus, a new Genesis is about to take place);
- the "voice from heaven" identifies and confirms Jesus ("Here is my servant … my chosen one with whom I am pleased" — Isaiah 42: 1, today's first reading; "The Lord said to me, 'You are my Son; this day I have begotten you'" — Psalm 2: 7).

Jesus' baptism at the Jordan becomes the moment of God's "anointing" of his Messiah (which means "anointed") for the work he is about to do. In the Spirit — *Namaste* — God rests and lives in Jesus.

In our own experience of baptism, the same *Namaste* of compassion, justice and peace that "descends" upon Jesus at his baptism by John descends and rests upon us, compelling us to take on the work of the Gospel. In baptism, we take on the name of "Christian" and embrace all that that holy name means: to live for others rather than for ourselves, in imitation of Christ. Our baptisms made each one of us the "servant" of today's readings: to bring forth in our world the justice, reconciliation and enlightenment of Christ, the "beloved Son" and "favor" of God.

Raise us up out of the waters of our baptism, O God,
and send down your Spirit to dwell within our hearts.
May we live lives of humble gratitude and integrity,
  always aware that your love is a power
  greater than anything we possess of our own;
may our struggle to live faithfully the Gospel
  of your beloved Son
make us worthy of our baptismal name Christian.

LENT

Ash Wednesday

"Your Father who sees what is hidden will repay you."
Matthew 6: 1–6, 16–18

Even now, says the Lord, return to me with your whole heart . . .
Joel 2: 12–18

We implore you, in Christ's name, be reconciled to God.
2 Corinthians 5: 20 – 6:2

Turn around!

They were driving to Chicago. As he cruised along, he passed his exit and his wife said, "Wasn't that our exit, honey?"

The man — being *male* — insisted, "No, I didn't miss anything."

"Maybe we should turn around," she said.

"Look, I'm driving the car," he said impatiently. "I know where I'm going. I know if I missed an exit."

"Let's stop and ask for directions," she suggested.

"There's no need for that," he snapped.

There was a long silence. He continued on, praying desperately for a sign — any sign — for Chicago. The signs they passed stopped reading Chicago and began marking Gary, Indiana.

"Honey! All the signs for Chicago have stopped; you're going the wrong way."

He gritted his teeth and opted for an exit. Hope for a sign to Chicago had faded.

His wife piped up one more time, "Honey, you're being ridiculous. Stop and turn around."

But he kept on, determined to prove her wrong. He would find his way without turning around.

But several hours and many miles later, he — with great humility — turned around.

She — with much grace — said nothing.

Today we begin the season for "turning around." In fact, the words repentance (Hebrew) and conversion (Latin) come from the same root: *to turn.* Lent (from the Anglo-Saxon word for *spring)* is the season for *turning:* The earth completes its spring "turning" toward the sun; we soon begin the "turning" of the ground for the spring planting.

The Lenten springtime is also a "turning" of our souls and spirits. The Spirit of God leads us into the Lenten wilderness to look back on the roads we have traveled so far and to realize the "turns" before us, as we have to make our way to God.

The three readings for Ash Wednesday all call us to a *turning* of perspective and attitude:

In today's Gospel, from his Sermon on the Mount, Jesus instructs his listeners on the Christian attitude and disposition toward prayer, fasting and almsgiving. Such acts are meaningful only if they are outward manifestations of the essential *turning* that has taken place within our hearts.

In the first reading, the prophet Joel calls the people of Judah to repent, to *turn* to the Lord with fasting, prayer and works of charity. A devastating invasion of locusts has ravaged Judah (around 400 BC). The prophet sees this catastrophe as a sign of the coming "Day of the Lord" and pleads with the community to turn away from their self-absorbed lives and re-turn to the God of mercy and graciousness.

The Church at Corinth is a deeply divided community. Some factions have challenged Paul himself and his mandate as an apostle. In his second letter to the Corinthians (today's second reading), Paul alternates between anger and compassion, between frustration and affection, in appealing for reconciliation and unity — for a re-*turn* to the one faith they all share as the Church of the Risen Christ.

Lent is a time to stop and check our bearings, to realize what turns we have to make along the crooked roads we travel. Repentance and conversion are not momentary experiences that are detached from our everyday lives; conversion and repentance are the never-completed, hard work of becoming, growing and *turning: turning away* from whatever unjustly and unfairly steals our time and energy and *turning towards* the loving embrace of family and friends; *turning away* from those idols of wealth and prestige that take the place of the Holy One in our lives and *turning towards* the things of God we hold in the depths of our hearts.

Lord God, may this day of ashes and prayer
be the first "turn" in our Lenten journey.
May we embrace your Spirit of selflessness and humility
to realize our need to "turn" things around,
to change the directions of our lives.
May our journey with you
    from the desert to the mount of transfiguration,
    from Jerusalem to Calvary,
be an experience of "turning" for us —
a "turning" from despair to hope,
a "turning" from barrenness to fullness,
a "turning" from death to life.

Filled with the Holy Spirit, Jesus was led by the Spirit into the desert for forty days to be tempted by the devil.

Luke 4: 1–13

The road through the desert

You have just been dumped — abandoned, betrayed, rejected by someone you loved and thought (hoped?) loved you. Now you have to put your life back together. You have to move on. Whichever road you take passes through the desert with Jesus.

It is the first day at a new school, the first day at a new job. *Do I belong here? Is this going to be a good fit? Can I make this work? Will the other kids like me? Can I play with these kids? What's for lunch?* The first day of any new adventure begins in the desert with Jesus.

Worry is part of a parent's job description. Are we up to the job of raising another human being? How can we raise a kid when we're not quite sure that we're adults yet? Are we doing right by our kids? Where do we find the strength and patience to keep loving our teenage sons and daughters despite their leveling "attitude," to keep reaching out to them in the face of their dismissive rolling eyes, to continue to wait up no matter how late the hour? Whether we realize it or not, to love a child is to dwell in the desert with Christ.

Every important decision we make in our lives takes place in the desert of doubt; every milestone, every watershed moment, begins in the wilderness of humility.

The Gospel for this First Sunday of Lent takes us into the desert with Christ. The desert as described by Luke is more accurately understood as a wilderness — a dangerous, uncharted place, inhabited by wild beasts and bandits, and (many believed) haunted by demons. The people of Jesus' time saw the desert as a place where one encountered the holy. Jesus embarks on his wilderness "retreat" as a time for discerning and understanding his mission as the Messiah. These forty days are marked by intense prayer and fasting — not out of a sense of penance but to focus totally on God and the Father's will for him.

The three temptations recounted in Luke's Gospel all confront Jesus with very human choices:

- "command this stone to become bread": Will Jesus use his power for his own gratification and acclaim or to accomplish the will of God?
- "All this will be yours, if you worship me": Will Jesus compromise the values of God to accommodate the values of the world?
- "throw yourself down from here": Will Jesus pray that God will do Jesus' will rather than Jesus seeking God's will? Will Jesus seek to make God into Jesus' image or seek to become what God calls him to be?

During this lonely and difficult time, Jesus comes to terms with the life that lay before him. Jesus then follows the Spirit obediently on to Galilee to begin his teaching ministry.

The same Spirit that led Jesus into the desert leads us into this 40-day "wilderness experience" of Lent. The Spirit prompts us to ask ourselves the same kind of questions, to begin to understand who we are and who we are becoming, to discern what God calls us to be as we journey to the dwelling place of God. Lent calls us into the desert of our hearts, into the silent wilderness within us where God speaks to us of hope and encouragement; the quiet wood where we clear our heads to realize what is right and good; the plateau from which we can see the path we should take if we are to become the people of justice and compassion we seek to become.

O God, lead us this Lent into the deserts of our hearts.
Let these days be a time
of discernment and discovery,
of resolution and conversion
for each of us.

May your Word be our bread
  during our wilderness journey;
may your light illuminate the treacherous turns
  of the road we walk;
may your grace and wisdom minister to us
  in our deserts of sadness and despair.

Second Sunday of Lent

While Jesus was praying, his face changed in appearance and his clothing became dazzling white. Moses and Elijah appeared in glory and spoke of his exodus that he was going to accomplish in Jerusalem.

Luke 9: 28–36
[Roman lectionary]

To become the person you once needed

When Sara became ill as a teenager, bulimia was not yet a household word. Filled with guilt at her uncontrollable behavior, she was taken to specialist after specialist until someone was able to identify the problem as something much more than teenage rebellion. Slowly she fought her way back from the edge. Sara was surrounded by many loving adults, but no one could understand why she was doing this to herself. She didn't understand it either. Sara fought her disease alone and managed to conquer it.

One day, the now happily married Sara read a story in her local newspaper about a new support group for those suffering from bulimia. Though long recovered from her own nightmare, she was intrigued by the idea of a support group and went to the meeting. It was a powerful experience. The desperately ill young people there touched her heart. While she felt unable to help them, she cared about them and continued attending the meetings. Other than saying she had bulimia as a girl, Sara revealed little about herself at the meetings; she sat quietly and listened to the stories of others.

As she was about to leave one of the sessions, Sara was stopped by a painfully thin girl who thanked her for coming and told her how much her presence meant to her. The girl's eyes filled with tears. Sara responded with her usual graciousness, but was puzzled. Sara could not recall ever speaking to this girl and did not even know her name.

As she drove home, Sara wondered how she could have forgotten something so important to someone else. She was almost home when it dawned on her.

Her husband, who met her at the front door, was surprised to see that she had been crying.

"Sara, what's wrong?" he asked.

A smile broke through her tears.

Walking into her husband's loving embrace, she said happily, "Harry, I've become the person I needed to meet."[1]

The lesson of the Transfiguration is that the Spirit of God exists within each one of us, enabling us to become the person God calls us to be. It is that same Spirit, that same "divinity," that Peter, James and John see in Jesus on the mount of the Transfiguration. That power of that sacred presence shines through us, as well, even when we do not notice. Like Sara, we can be a blessing to others, simply by being who we are.

Luke's account of the transfiguration is filled with Old Testament imagery (the voice heard in the cloud, for example) that echoes the Exodus event. In Luke's Gospel, the transfiguration takes place after Jesus' instructions to his followers on the cost of discipleship. It is a turning point in the Gospel: the beginning of a new exodus, Jesus' difficult "Passover" from crucifixion to resurrection.

As his disciples, we, too, are called to experience the Passover and exodus of Jesus — an exodus from the impermanence of this world and our own sinfulness to the reign of God, a "passing over" from this life to the life of God. In our own "Passovers" and "exoduses," in our own "transfigurations" from confusion to understanding, in our own experiences of death and resurrection, we become for others, as Sara became for one young bulimic, a mirror of the Spirit of God in our midst.

O Christ, the very Light and Word of God,
may this Lent be an experience of transfiguration
for us.
Illuminate our spirits

that we may rediscover the sense of the sacred
   within ourselves.
May that sacredness enable us to see
beyond our own needs, wants and interests
so that we may set about to transfigure
   our lives and our world
in your compassion, justice and forgiveness.

[In the Common Lectionary, this Gospel is read on the Sunday before Ash Wednesday.]

Second Sunday of Lent

"Jerusalem, Jerusalem, the city that kills the prophets and stones those who are sent to it! How often have I desired to gather your children as a hen gathers her brood under her wings, and you were not willing!"

Luke 13: 31–35
[Common lectionary]

Semmelweis' folly

You probably have never heard of Ignaz Semmelweis — yet he is responsible for one of the most important innovations in health care. And it cost him his medical career and, some believe, his life.

Doctor Semmelweis was an obstetrician in 19th-century Austria. Puerperal fever was killing 13 percent of the women who gave birth in his Vienna hospital. A close friend died from an infection after accidentally cutting himself with a knife while performing an autopsy. Semmelweis found that his friend died of symptoms similar to the women who died of puerperal fever. The physician began to suspect that the doctors themselves were bringing the infection to the mothers — he noticed that doctors often went directly from dissecting corpses in the morgue to examining mothers in the maternity ward. He began to make a connection that would not be confirmed for another decade: that germs cause disease.

That's when Semmelweis proposed a bold experiment: that doctors and nurses wash their hands before treating their patients.

His colleagues were indignant at Semmelweis' hypothesis. How dare this young nobody doctor make such a suggestion to physicians far more experienced and knowledgeable! But Doctor Semmelweis stubbornly pushed and pushed. Some doctors ridiculed Semmelweis by scrubbing their hands with great histrionics, making fun of Semmelweis' simplistic solution.

But the dying stopped. Doctor Semmelweis' simple suggestion, now standard procedure in all hospitals, saved millions and millions of lives — including yours and mine and your children and your children's children.

Yet, rather than being hailed for his discovery, Doctor Semmelweis continued to be deeply resented and excoriated. Doctor Semmelweis, in turn, publicly denounced the medical establishment for their irresponsibility and indifference to the deaths of their poor patients. He was eventually forced out of the hospital and Austria itself. He finished his career in a small provincial hospital in Hungary where he died a broken and disillusioned man.

The experience of Ignaz Semmelweis' rejection by the medical community mirrors Israel's figurative and literal stoning of the prophet that Jesus laments in today's Gospel. Jesus identifies with the fate of the prophets who have suffered and died for their forthright but unpopular proclaiming of God's reign. Their witness to the mercy and compassion of God has cost them dearly. Jerusalem has become the antithesis of God's "city of peace."

In our own Jerusalems, we try to destroy what we fear or do not understand; like Herod, who has had enough of Jesus' harsh but on-target admonitions and wants to kill him, we dismiss or discredit anything that threatens our own comfortable view of the world; we discourage or frustrate any change that will upset the haven of safety we have created for ourselves. But faith is a vision much greater than ourselves, a spirit of servanthood that embraces all men and women as brothers and sisters, a sense of justice and hope that seeks reconciliation, forgiveness and compassion above all else.

As Doctor Semmelweis tragically discovered, giving witness to the truth, proclaiming justice, can be costly. Our own prophecy of the things of God can subject us to misunderstanding, suspicion, abuse, intimidation and ridicule; living the principles of the Gospel can be discouraging, isolating and humiliating. Yet every one of us who claims to be a disciple of Jesus and a witness of his Resurrection is called to pay whatever price is demanded for the sake of the reign of God.

Make our homes your dwelling place, O God;
come and transform our Jerusalems into
"cities of peace,"
where your justice and mercy reign.
Send your Christ to gather us together
in love and forgiveness,
making us prophets of your compassion
to our communities.

Third Sunday of Lent

"A person had a fig tree planted in his orchard: 'For three years now I have come in search of fruit on this fig tree but have found none. So cut it down. Why should I exhaust the soil?' The gardener replied, 'Sir, leave it for this year also, and I shall cultivate the ground around it and fertilize it; it may bear fruit in the future.' "

Luke 13: 1–9

The Metamorphosis

It is one of the most bizarre tales in literature: Franz Kafka's surrealistic *The Metamorphosis.* Gregor Samsa, a young salesman, wakes up one morning and discovers that he has been transformed into a giant, ugly bug. As the days wear on, Gregor and his mother, father and sister struggle to adjust to their son and brother's predicament. Sadly, Gregor loses his sense of humanity and fights to feel love and companionship with his ever-more estranged family.

But the one thing that gives Gregor peace is the beautiful music his sister Anna plays on her violin in the evening. Trapped in the body of a beetle, Gregor listens to the piece and wonders: *Could I really be an animal if music stirs me this way?*

Today's Gospel is about finding that spark of humanity within us that can be lost in times of despair and anguish. Despite the struggle and tragedy that can cut down our lives in disappointment and despair, God continues to plant in our midst opportunities to start over, to try again, to rework things, to move beyond our hurt and pain to make things right.

The belief prevailed in Jesus' time that disasters and catastrophes were signs of God's anger against sinful individuals or people: those massacred in the temple by Pilate's soldiers during what the Romans perceived as a "revolt" and the workers who were killed when the tower they were building collapsed must have been horrible sinners, people thought.

Nonsense, Jesus says. In this present age, neither good fortune nor calamity are indicators of one's favor or disfavor with God. In the age to come, God will judge the hearts of every soul, regardless of their situation in life.

The parable of the fig tree has been called the "Gospel of the second chance." The vinedresser pleads for the tree, asking that it be given another year to bear fruit. We always live in the hope and mercy of God who keeps giving us "second chances" to rise from the ashes of sin to rebuild and reform our lives. God is the ever-patient gardener who gives every "fig tree" all the time, care and attention it needs to harvest.

The fig tree is an invitation to hope in the unlimited love and mercy of God. In God, we are able to discover the "music" within ourselves that makes us loving, compassionate human beings; in God, we are able to realize our lives' harvest.

God of new beginnings,
you constantly call us back to you —
You transform every death into resurrection;
you are never satisfied with endings
but always enable us to begin again and again.
God of second and third chances,
you are the ever-patient gardener
who nurtures our broken and dried branches
in the water of your love
and the food of your compassion.
Help us to rekindle within our broken spirits
that spark that gives us hope;
open our souls to hear the music of your Spirit within us;
nourish us by your grace and nourish us by your love
that we may realize the harvest of your justice
and peace in our lives.

Fourth Sunday of Lent

The parable of the prodigal: "While he was still a long way off, his father caught sight of him, and was filled with compassion. He ran to his son, embraced him and kissed him."

Luke 15: 1–3, 11–32

Waiting for your child

Mom and Dad wait. It's well past their bed time, but sleep is out of the question. Their teenage son is out with friends. Curfew is eleven. They know he'll be home on time — sure enough, they hear the door slam exactly at eleven. Coming into the living room, he asks, "Why did you wait up?" Trying to be cool, they say "We weren't waiting up — we just wanted to see the end of this movie." Then it's off to bed for everyone, home and family once again complete and at peace.

Mom and Dad wait. Everything has been a blur since the call came: Meghan was crossing the street on her way home from school and a car came out of nowhere and the driver didn't see her and someone called 911 and … After hours of surgery, they sit by Meghan's hospital bed, their precious little girl hooked up to a wall of blinking monitors. For the time being, this small hospital room is home.

Mom and Dad wait. The angry words still resonate in the house. Over time, this storm, too, like the hundreds of other squalls that rock a family, will blow over. Until then, Mom and Dad put aside their own heartbreak and ready themselves to be the forgiving and welcoming parents when angry son or put-upon daughter returns because that's what you do when you're a Mom and Dad.

Mom and Dad wait. One afternoon, their son hopped on his bike to go to a friend's house but never arrived. The days became weeks, the weeks months. The police are baffled, but Mom and Dad never give up. They organize volunteers to search. They appear on television and radio, set up a website and listen to anyone, from profilers to psychics, who might help. They quit their jobs, deplete their savings and borrow against their retirement to find their child. For Mom and Dad, it has been one long, continuous day since that afternoon weeks ago. But when you're a parent, the last thing you surrender is hope.

The love of a parent for his/her child is a remarkable thing. Children often have no idea how much their parents do and would do for them; many good parents don't realize what their love for their sons and daughters enable them to do.

In the parable of the prodigal (a story found only in Luke's Gospel), Jesus holds up the boy's father as a model of compassion and reconciliation. Note that when he catches sight of his son in the distance, the father *runs* to greet and embrace him before the prodigal can even open his mouth to begin his carefully rehearsed speech; the father welcomes his son home with no recriminations, no conditions, no rancor. The father has never lost hope in his son's return; his love has survived the hurt and anguish of his son's leaving.

A parent's love is the very reflection of God's love for each one of us — love that always welcomes back, love that reconciles and heals, love that perseveres through every hurt and heartache, through every long day and night of waiting.

Merciful God, make us vessels of your mercy.
When we are lost,
  may your mercy enable us to find our way back;
when we are searching for our lost loved ones,
  may your mercy support us in our anxiety;
when we are hurt and angry,
  may your mercy be a well from which we draw
  from your abundant patience and understanding.

Fifth Sunday of Lent

"Let the one among you who is without sin be the first to throw a stone at her."

John 8: 1–11
[Roman lectionary]

"Welcome to heaven. Your table is ready."

There was a dedicated old priest who had always wondered what the real difference was between heaven and hell. One day, he had a dream in which God showed him.

First, God showed him hell. The old priest was flabbergasted to find no flames, no horned pointy-tailed devils — only crowds of angry people pressing around long, wooden picnic tables. At each place was a large wooden bowl of food and 10-foot-long wooden spoons. By pushing and shoving into place at the table, the angry people managed to get their long spoons into the bowls, but they were unable to turn the spoons around and get them into their mouths. Their frustration and the accompanying bitterness and bickering were sheer hell!

Then the old priest was given a glimpse of heaven. He was amazed to discover the same massive wooden picnic tables, the same huge wooden bowls of food, and the same 10-foot-long wooden spoons. But in heaven there was a spirit of peace, thoughtfulness, even joy. In heaven, the people were feeding one another.

Today's Gospel centers on the need to change our own hearts before we demand the conversion of others. To enter the kingdom of God, to realize the reign of God among us in the here and now, we must embrace a new attitude toward God and one another, an attitude based on compassion, generosity, forgiveness, and justice; an attitude that seeks to lift up the fallen rather than self-justification in the failings of others, an attitude not centered in self but in the common good.

The story of the adulteress, a later addition to John's Gospel (probably added in the third century), is a cherished tale from the then rich oral history of Jesus' life. Once again, the scribes and Pharisees set up a trap to discredit Jesus. According to the Mosaic code, adultery was considered among the gravest of sins, punishable by death; but the law of the Roman occupiers forbade the Jewish authorities to impose and carry out the death sentence on anyone. The dilemma facing Jesus, then, is this: If Jesus condemns the woman, he undermines his own teachings on forgiveness and puts him in conflict with the Roman authority; if he does not condemn her, he breaks faith with the covenant Law.

Jesus' response to their hypocrisy challenges the Jews' understanding of judgment and authority: God reserves the role of judging others to himself; to us belongs the work of forgiveness and reconciliation. God's commandments are addressed to each one of us as individuals to keep; we are called to judge our own actions and pass sentence on our own lives. While the scribes and Pharisees view authority as a license to criticize, censure and condemn this woman, Jesus sees authority as a gift for transforming her life and reconciling her with God.

Admittedly, the Pharisees and scribes' approach to morality does have a certain appeal: root it out and cut it down. But Jesus challenges them to a more lasting, permanent conversion:

Put down your stones of indignation and anger and look to your hearts, to that place within every one of us, where good and evil meet. Understand the disappointments, the despair, the selfishness that drive you to sin. Realize the hurt, the pain, the destruction others suffer because of your own sin. Put aside your rationalizations and excuses and embrace the love and mercy of God, who knows our hearts better than we do ourselves.

Confronting the demons of the world must begin with confronting the demons within our own hearts: We cannot lift up the fallen until we realize that we, too, are fallen; we cannot raise others to health and hope until we seek our own healing; we cannot pass sentence on others until we judge our own lives. Jesus calls us to realize the old priest's vision of heaven in our own time and place: Heaven dawns in the humility to feed one another from the bounty of God's table; hell is the hunger and poverty of selfishness and acrimony.

Father of forgiveness,
make us a people of compassion.
Give us the courage to reach out to those
who fall along the road we all travel,
that we may transform what is evil
into the reflection of your love.
Humble us with the grace to seek forgiveness
when we fall
so that we may replace the hurt we have caused
with healing and reconciliation.

The parable of the vineyard owner and murderous tenants: "The stone that the builders rejected has become the cornerstone … "

Luke 20: 9–19
[Common lectionary]

The legend of bamboo

The Thais have a wonderful legend about the bamboo plant:

When the great garden of the earth was first planted, Bamboo was the most beautiful plant of all, the favorite flower of God, the Master of the Garden. In one corner of the earth there were some dry fields. A spring of water was in the center of the fields, but its water could not reach the dry earth. So God took Bamboo and cut him down; the Master then hacked off his branches and stripped off his leaves, cleaved him in two and cut out his heart. Then God gently carried Bamboo to the fresh water spring and, putting one end of broken Bamboo in the spring and the other end into the water channel in the dry field, the Master gently laid down his beloved Bamboo. The clear waters raced joyously down the channel of Bamboo's torn body into the waiting fields. The rice was planted, the shoots grew and the harvest came.

On that day, Bamboo, once so glorious in its stately beauty, became more glorious in his brokenness and humility.

There is no doubt among Jesus' hearers about the meaning of the allegory in today's Gospel. Using the image of the vineyard, a familiar symbol for Israel used by many of the prophets and the psalmist, Jesus portrays the empty, self-centered faith of the scribes and chief priests. First, they (the tenants of the land entrusted to them by God the landowner) ignore the prophets calling them to return to God (the vineyard owner) the harvest of justice and compassion God has planted; then they reject John the Baptizer, who is murdered at the hands of the evil Herod; and now the stage is set for their destroying God's own Son. But Jesus warns that the evil tenants will be crushed under the weight of the "cornerstone" they have rejected, the stone that will be the foundation of God's new city. Jesus' parable is met with deep resentment and outrage by the religious leaders who hear it.

Like the legend of Bamboo, Jesus' life is a story of how a spirit of humble servanthood can transform barrenness into harvest, evil into good, selfishness into justice, death into life. In the person of his Son, God makes his home among our own small "vineyards"; he lives our lives and embraces our fears and hardships, showing us how, in his humility and compassion, to transform and re-create our lives in his compassion. In his broken body, he restores humanity to the life and love of God.

Christ asks all of us who would be his disciples to embrace the role of the servant Bamboo, emptying ourselves of our own needs and wants and self-importance for the sake of others, realizing the profound truth that we receive only in giving, that greatness is found only in humility and service, that resurrection is possible only in suffering and death.

Father, help us to embrace the example
of your Son's spirit of servanthood—
that in our humble dying to self,
we may rise to new life and hope for all.
By your grace that enables us to do
    what we don't think we can do,
by your wisdom that shows us the way
    through the most treacherous places,
by your light that illuminates the darkest places,
may we transform our gardens and vineyards into places
where your justice blossoms and your peace abounds.

Sunday of the Lord's Passion: Palm Sunday

The Blessing and Procession of Palms

As Jesus rode along, the people were spreading their cloaks on the road; and now as he was approaching the slope of the Mount of Olives, the whole multitude of his disciples began to praise God aloud with joy for all the mighty deeds they had seen.

Luke 19: 28–40

Giving Christ the coat off your back

Notice something missing in Luke's version of Jesus' entry into Jerusalem on Palm Sunday?

No palm branches.

Unlike Matthew and Mark's accounts, Luke makes no mention of palm branches being waved or Hosannas being sung (instead, the crowds repeat the angels' song of "peace" and "glory" from Luke's Christmas narrative). Typical of his Gospel, Luke's account of Jesus' entry into Jerusalem portrays the coming of a Messiah of peace. The kings of antiquity rode horses when they came in war, but entering Jerusalem on an ass indicates the "kingship" of peace and service that Jesus has come to exercise.

In Luke's account of Jesus' Palm Sunday entry into the holy city, the people place their single most important article of clothing — their cloaks — along Jesus' path. A cloak was the most expensive article of clothing one possessed — most people owned only one that was constantly mended and never discarded. For the poorest of the poor, a cloak was more than an article of clothing: it was their shelter and home. The holy poor of Luke's narrative place all that they have at the disposal of the Messiah-king.

This Sunday of the Lord's Passion is about "emptying" oneself in order to be filled with the love of God (from today's second reading: Paul's beautiful hymn to the Servant Christ from Philippians). The people of Jerusalem "empty" themselves of their most precious possession to welcome into their midst the Anointed One of God and his reign of peace; Christ empties himself of his very divinity in obedience to the Father's will that humanity should be reconciled to God through his passion.

To be disciples of the Messiah Jesus is to put aside our "cloaks" of comfort and fear in which we wrap ourselves in order to embrace Christ's spirit of humility and selflessness, to "empty" ourselves of our pride and our own wants and needs in order to become vessels of God's life and love.

The Reading of the Passion

The criminal said, "Jesus, remember me when you come into your kingdom." Jesus replied to him, "Amen, I say to you, today you will be with me in Paradise." Jesus cried out in a loud voice: "Father, into your hands I commend my spirit … "

Luke 22: 14 – 23: 56

"Paradise Now"

It is a scene found only in Luke's Gospel:

As he hangs in agony on the cross, Jesus is taunted by the bystanders. Even one of the criminals crucified with him joins in the jeering.

But the other criminal will have none of it. Luke doesn't explain how or why, but something opens up within the heart of the "good thief." Despite his own impending death, the criminal realizes the injustice of Jesus' execution and senses God both with and within the man hanging next to him. He rebukes the other criminal, admitting that both he and the other criminal are guilty but that Jesus is innocent. And then, in a plea that resounds through the centuries, he turns to Jesus and asks, "Jesus, remember me when you come into your kingdom."

The dying Jesus responds out of compassion and mercy. "Today you will be with me in Paradise."

This is the Jesus we have followed throughout Luke's Gospel. Luke's Jesus possesses a sense of confidence and peace in the mercy of the God he proclaims. The Jesus of Luke's account readily welcomes into his company the poor, the outcast, the sinner; women, considered less than second-class citizens in the world of the time, play prominent roles in Luke's narrative. It is Luke's Jesus who makes a Samaritan traveler the model of compassion in his parable; it is Luke's Jesus who calls his listeners to embrace the example of the patient father who lovingly welcomes back his prodigal son; it is Luke's Jesus who seeks the hospitality of the despised tax collector Zacchaeus; it is Luke's Jesus who is moved with compassion for the widow at Naim.

The Jesus of Luke's passion story continues to embody that same spirit of compassion, forgiveness and selflessness. Only in Luke's Gospel does Jesus heal the severed ear of the high priest's servant. In Luke's version, Jesus does not rebuke his disciples for falling asleep during the garden watch. Luke's Passion account includes that poignant scene when Jesus, struggling under the weight of the cross, tells the women of Jerusalem not to be concerned for him but for themselves: if such injustice can befall the innocent Jesus (the "green wood"), what horrors await an unrepentant ("dry") Jerusalem?

And, once at the Place of the Skull, Jesus' crucifixion becomes an occasion for sacred forgiveness: he prays that God will forgive his executioners and promises paradise to the penitent thief crucified with him. Even Jesus' final words on the cross are not words of abandonment but of hope: Luke's Crucified does not cry out Psalm 22 (as he does in Matthew and Mark's narrative) but prays Psalm 31: 5–6: "Father, into your hands I commend my spirit." Luke's Jesus is the Suffering Servant whose death for the sake of humanity will be exalted in the Resurrection three days hence.

Luke portrays a Christ of extraordinary compassion and love, who forgives those who betray and destroy him, who consoles those who grieve for him, whose final breaths give comfort and hope to a condemned criminal who seeks reconciliation with God. The Paradise he promises the good thief is the kingdom of God that he has been preaching since he made his way down the mount of the transfiguration: God's reign of love, justice and reconciliation, has come.

"Today you will be with me in Paradise" — every act of generosity and mercy resonates with that promise and springs from the same source. In imitating Christ's mercy, in taking up his work of reconciliation, in struggling to be salt for the earth and light for the world, we profess our belief that Paradise not only exists in the future but exists now, hidden in the present.

And Jesus promises to be with us in Paradise, not just after our own deaths, but today, in this very moment, in the Paradise we open up in our households and communities.

Christ our Redeemer,
may we not only remember your passion, death
  and resurrection this Holy Week,
but may we enter, heart and soul,
into your "Passover" from death to life.
May the example of your selfless compassion
guide our faltering steps as we struggle to follow you
    from Jerusalem to the upper room,
    from agony to trial,
    from crucifixion to burial.
May we empty ourselves of our own hurts and wants
in order to become vessels of your mercy and
  consolation for others;
may we take up our crosses as you took up yours
in the certain hope that our experiences of crucifixion
    for the sake of justice and integrity
may be transformed into the vindication of Easter.

The Easter Triduum

"If I, your Teacher and Lord, washed your feet, then you must wash each other's feet."

John 13: 1–15

Final gifts

In the summer, she learned her illness was terminal. She was not surprised. She was scared, of course, but she accepted her fate. She knew exactly the course the disease would take.

So, while she was still able, she went to work — planning, shopping, wrapping. When she was finished, she took her children and grandchildren on one last family trip to Disney World. Everyone had a ball. A week before Christmas, with her family at her side, she died.

On Christmas morning, they found the boxes around the tree. She had spent those last weeks selecting and purchasing the best Christmas presents she could think of. For the newborn grandchild, she had made a beautiful christening gown. For the teenage granddaughter who would go to her first prom in the spring, a small box contained a pearl necklace. For the six-year-old grandson, his first bike. A special box for her daughter included a beautiful album of family photographs she had prepared, along with her grandmother's favorite pendant. For her son, she had her late husband's watch repaired and cleaned — it shined like the day she bought it for her husband for their wedding 55 years before. She had spent hours choosing and making afghans and scarves and buying and wrapping CDs and DVDs and other gifts for each member of the family.

Mom's last gifts were her best. In those gifts and the love that went into them, Mom would always be with them.

Tonight, Jesus, facing the reality of his death, leaves his followers his last two gifts. He leaves them the sacrament of his body and blood in the bread and wine of the new Passover — but he also leaves them the gift of the towel and the basin, his last "parable" on humble servanthood.

The centerpiece of John's Gospel account of the Last Supper is the *mandatum* — from the Latin word for "commandment," from which comes the traditional title for this evening, *Maundy* Thursday. At the Passover seder, the night before he died, Jesus established a new Passover to celebrate God's covenant with the new Israel. The special character of this second covenant is the *mandatum* of the washing of the feet — to love one another as we have been loved by Christ.

(John makes no mention of the establishment of the Eucharist in his account of the Last Supper. Chapters 14, 15 and 16 recount Jesus' last instructions to his disciples, followed by his "high priestly prayer" in chapter 17. The Johannine theology of the Eucharist is detailed in the "bread of life" discourse following the multiplication of the loaves and fish at Passover, in chapter 6 of his Gospel.)

Jesus, who revealed the wonders of God in stories about mustard seeds, fishing nets and ungrateful children, on this last night of his life — as we know life — leaves his small band of disciples his most beautiful parable: *As I have washed your feet like a slave, so you must wash the feet of each other and serve one another. As I have loved you without limit or condition, so you must love one another without limit or condition. As I am about to suffer and die for you, so you must suffer and, if necessary, die for one another.* Tonight's parable is so simple, but its lesson is so central to what being a disciple of Christ is all about. When inspired by the love of Christ, the smallest act of service done for another takes on extraordinary dimensions.

In the bread and wine of the Eucharist — the new Passover seder of the Church, the new Israel — Christ asks us to become the Eucharist we receive: the embodiment of God's compassion, mercy and justice.

In his last two gifts to his Church, given out of a love too profound and deep to fully grasp, Christ remains with us always.

Father in heaven,
may we accept with humility and gratitude
the gifts your Son leaves us this night.
May we joyfully accept the towel and basin
to become footwashers for one another;
may our putting aside our own wants and needs
to wash the feet of others
make us worthy to become Jesus' second gift,
the gift of himself in the Eucharist.

Good Friday

It was preparation day for Passover, and it was about noon.

John 18: 1 – 19: 42

Preparation day

It was a very busy day — the day before a major holiday. It was as busy as the day before Thanksgiving or Christmas Eve. There was shopping to be done and dinner preparations to complete. The house needed to be cleaned and guests to be welcomed. Businesses had customers to serve and transactions to complete before the start of the holiday at sunset.

In his account of Jesus' passion, the evangelist John notes that it was the preparation day before the Sabbath — and that year it was also the Passover feast. Everyone was busy — too busy to notice what was taking place in "official" Jerusalem. In John's telling, there are no taunting crowds demanding Jesus' blood. Jesus' arrest and trial, taking place in the middle of the night, are "handled" by Pilate, his soldiers and the Jewish authorities. So few people witness Jesus' death that John identifies them by name.

Some Scripture scholars believe that John's account is the most accurate description of what happened on Good Friday. The death of Jesus was not the headline of the day in Jerusalem. The depiction of massive crowds clamoring for Jesus' death in the other three Gospels was probably not the case — Pilate and his forces would not have countenanced that. To them, the Jesus "incident" was a Jewish matter that concerned them only in so far as it could disturb public order. As was their modus operandi, they took care of it as they would any other problem — directly, quickly, mercilessly. And so, scholars conclude, Jesus died alone, quietly, and out of the way.

So while Jerusalem went about the business of Passover, God was putting into motion a second Passover:

As a brisk trade in the buying and selling of lambs for Passover was taking place all over the city, the Lamb of God was slain just outside the gates.

While preparations for the Passover seder continued, the new Passover was completed on a cross planted on a hill.

During the Jewish community's celebration of their journey from slavery to nationhood, God was calling his people to a new exodus from death to life.

This Good Friday continues to be a day of preparation. The events of this day are not an end in themselves but the means to a much greater event: God completes the work of his second Genesis, in which he re-creates humankind in the Paschal mystery.

This Good Friday is God's calling us to a second Exodus journey, marked in the slaying of his Son, the Lamb, who becomes for us the new Passover seder — today is our exodus from the slavery of sin to the freedom of compassion and forgiveness, our "passing over" from this life to the life of God.

Today our own city carries on its business, nearly oblivious to what we gather in an austere church to remember.

Jesus hangs on his cross and the world walks by.

On this busy spring Good Friday, God transforms humanity to its very core.

And humanity seems too busy to notice.

Compassionate God,
we stand before the cross,
humbled by your love,
chastened by the injustice and hatred that brought
your Son to it.
May Jesus' cross re-create us
in your compassion and forgiveness;
may his Gospel be the fire and cloud
that lead us in our exodus
from the slavery of sin and death
to the freedom of your justice and peace;
may his "Passover" be our "Passover"
from this life to life in your presence forever.

"Why do you look for the living among the dead? He is not here, but has risen. Remember what he said to you while he was still in Galilee, that the Son of Man must be handed over to sinners and be crucified, and rise on the third day."

Luke 24: 1–12

The risen One in your midst

And so the story goes:

The women of Jesus' company, whose compassion outweighs practicality, get up early the day after the Passover Sabbath to finish the job of burying Jesus. There they find the stone rolled away (how they planned to pry that boulder from the tomb's entrance is one of the great not-thought-through questions in all of Scripture). The tomb is empty. Two angels greet them.

Why do you seek the living among the dead?

What a strange — and somewhat chiding — thing to say to these poor, terrified, well-intentioned women.

But it's the central question of this long night.

He is not here. He is risen. It's not over. It's only begun. Don't think you can come here and hide. Go into the streets and look for him. Go to the prisons and soup kitchens. Go to the ghettos and hamlets. Go home to your families. He is there among your spouse and children, your coworkers and friends, your classmates and teammates. Go! Beat it! Get on with it! The best part of the story is ahead of you![1]

Remember what he said to you, the angels said.

Remember — not the mere recollection of a previous conversation but to understand with new and deepened insight the meaning of a past action and bringing its power and meaning into the present. It is in such creative and living "remembering" that the Church of the Resurrection is formed.

Typical of Luke, women — who possessed no true autonomy, whose testimony was considered of little value before a Jewish court — are the first proclaimers of the Easter Gospel. Sure enough, the disciples refuse to believe their wild story (in his original Greek text, the physician Luke describes the women's story as the excited babbling of a fevered and insane mind). Peter alone goes to investigate; Luke writes that Peter is "amazed" at what he sees, but still does not understand what has happened.

The work of remembering, the ministry of telling the story that has now become Gospel ("good news"), now begins at the empty tomb. The angels chide us to abandon the tombs in which we bury ourselves and challenge us to discover fulfillment in living a life centered beyond ourselves; the angels drive us out of the lifeless cemeteries where we hide in order to embrace the love of Christ present in family and community. Easter dares us to look around the rocks we stumble over and find the path of peace and forgiveness. Jesus has been raised up from the dead — he is not bound by burial cloths of hopelessness and cynicism; he is no longer entombed by fear and distrust; his cross is not the dead wood of shame and ridicule but the first branches of a harvest of compassion and justice for everyone of every time and place.

Jesus is no longer in the tomb.

So why are we?

Father, tonight we celebrate the empty tomb
of your Son —
your ultimate promise of hope, of life, of love
to humanity.
May the joy of this night give us the grace and hope
to abandon the tombs we create for ourselves
and bring the resurrection into this life of ours;
to renew and re-create our world in the light
of the Risen Christ;
to proclaim in every moment of our lives
the Gospel of the Holy One:
Christ Jesus who has died, who has risen,
and who comes again!

Easter

Easter Sunday

On the first day of the week, Mary of Magdala came to the tomb early in the morning, while it was still dark, and saw the stone removed from the tomb. So she ran and went to Simon Peter and to the other disciple whom Jesus loved, and told them. "They have taken the Lord from the tomb, and we don't know where they put him."

John 20: 1–9

A *real* Easter egg

A small chick begins the long journey to birth. The not-yet-a-bird weighs little more than air; its beak and claws are barely pinpricks. The bird-to-be is in its own little world: protected by the rigid shell, warmed by the mother hen's body, nourished by the nutrients within the egg's membrane.

But then the chick begins the work of being born. Over several days the chick keeps picking and picking until it can break out from its narrow world — and into an incomparably wider one.

But for this to happen, the egg has to go to pieces. New life demands shattering the old.

That is the *real* Easter egg. Not a complete egg dyed and painted with so many designs and colors. Not an egg that has been hardboiled, impossible to shatter. Not an egg made of chocolate.

The real Easter egg is shattered and destroyed. The real Easter egg exists in broken pieces. The real Easter egg is cracked open, yielding new life that has taken flight.

John's Easter Gospel centers on the "broken egg" of the story — the empty tomb. John says nothing of earthquakes or angels. His account begins before daybreak. It was the belief of the time that the spirit of the deceased hovered around the tomb for three days after burial; Mary Magdalene was therefore following the

Jewish custom of visiting the tomb during this three-day period. Discovering that the stone has been moved away, Mary runs to tell Peter and the others. Peter and the "other disciple" race to get there and look inside.

Note the different reactions of the three: Mary Magdalene fears that someone has "taken" Jesus' body; Peter does not know what to make of the news; but the "other" disciple — the model of faithful discernment in John's Gospel — immediately understands what has taken place. So great is the disciple's love and so deep is his faith that all of Jesus' strange remarks and mysterious references now become clear to him.

Like the struggle of the chick to free itself from its egg to embrace a much bigger world beyond it, we struggle to break out of a world that we perceive is going to pieces; we pick away at an existence that leaves us unsatisfied and unfulfilled. The promise of the empty tomb is that we can break out of our self-contained little worlds and take flight into a world that is not limited by our egos, our fears, our hurts; a world where peace and justice, respect and understanding reign; a world illuminated by hope and warmed by love; a world that extends beyond time and place into the forever of God's dwelling place.

Today we stand, with Peter and John and Mary, at the entrance of the "broken" tomb; with them, we struggle with what it means: The Christ who challenged us to love one another is risen and walks among us! All that he taught — compassion, love, forgiveness, reconciliation, sincerity, selflessness for the sake of others — is vindicated and affirmed in God's raising him up. The empty tomb should not only console us and elate us, it should challenge us to embrace the life of the Gospel. With Easter faith, we can awaken the promise of the empty tomb in every place and moment we encounter on our journey through this life.

God of limitless love and unfathomable goodness,
let the good news of the angels at the empty tomb
resound in our everyday lives.
May our struggle to live your Son's Spirit
of humility and compassion

enable us to break out of our own tombs
  of fear, despair and self-centeredness.
Let the Alleluia we sing this Easter
  ring out in every day and season
as we await the fulfillment of your Easter promise
  in our lives.

[NOTE: *The Gospel from the Easter Vigil may be read on Easter Sunday.*]

"Peace be with you. As the Father has sent me, so I send you." And when he said this he breathed upon them and said to them, "Receive the Holy Spirit ... " The other disciples told Thomas: "We have seen the Lord!" But he said to them, "Unless I see the mark of the nails in his hands, and put my finger in the mark of his nails and my hand in his side, I will not believe."

John 20: 19–31

Act 2

The Gospel for the Second Sunday of Easter (in all three years of the Lectionary cycle) is Act 2 of John's Easter drama.

Scene 1 takes place on Easter night. The terrified disciples are huddled together behind locked doors. Because of their association with the criminal Jesus, they are marked men. The Risen Jesus appears in their midst with his greeting of "peace." John clearly has the Genesis story in mind when the evangelist describes Jesus as "breathing" the Holy Spirit on his disciples: Just as God created man and woman by breathing life into them (Genesis 2: 7), the Risen Christ re-creates humankind by breathing the new life of the Holy Spirit upon the eleven.

The "peace" that Christ gives his new Church is not a sedative of good feeling or the simple absence of conflict or hostility. Christ's peace is active and transforming; it re-creates and renews. It is peace that is born of gratitude and humility, peace that values the hopes and dreams and needs of another over one's own, peace that welcomes back the lost, heals the brokenhearted, and respects the dignity of every man, woman and child as a son and daughter of God. Christ's peace is hard work; creating and maintaining the peace of Christ requires focused and determined action.

We trace our roots as a church to that Easter night. Jesus' "breathing" his spirit of peace and reconciliation upon his frightened disciples transformed them into a new creation, the Church. Jesus' gift of peace and his entrusting to his disciples the work of forgiveness defines the very identity of a church, a parish, a community of faith: to accept one another, to affirm one another, to support one another as God has done for us in the Risen Christ. What brought the Eleven and the first Christians together as a community — unity of heart, missionary witness, prayer, works of charity, a commitment to reconciliation and forgiveness — no less powerfully binds us to one another as the Church of the Risen Christ today.

In scene 2 of today's Gospel, the disciples excitedly tell the just-returned Thomas of what they had seen. Thomas responds to the news with understandable skepticism. Thomas had expected the cross (see John 11: 16 and 14: 5) — and no more.

The climactic third scene takes place one week later, with Jesus' second appearance to the assembled community — this time with Thomas present. He invites Thomas to examine his wounds and to "believe." Christ's blessing in response to Thomas' profession of faith exalts the faith of every Christian of every age who "believes without seeing," who realizes and celebrates the presence of the Risen Christ in their midst by living lives of Gospel compassion, justice and forgiveness. In raising his beloved Son from the dead, God also raises our spirits to the realization of the totality and limitlessness of his love for us.

While "doubting Thomas" will take his lumps from many pulpits this Sunday, his reaction is understandable. It is natural to approach any degree of change with skepticism and doubt. Whatever is new we greet initially with a healthy dose of skepticism; whatever challenges our usual way of doing things is rejected out of hand and scorned; whatever threatens our safe, comfortable approach to life must be neutralized before it can turn our world upside down. We have all been disappointed, bamboozled and ridiculed too many times. There's more than a little "doubting Thomas" in all of us.

Easter's empty tomb calls us to move beyond the betrayals and injustices we have endured that have instilled that dose of cynicism and doubt within our psyches. With an openness of heart and generosity of spirit, with perseverant faith in God's ever-present grace, wonderful things are possible, dreams worthy of our hope can be realized, resurrection can take place in our own time and place. As Thomas experiences, Easter transforms our crippling sense of skepticism and cynicism into a sense of trust and hope in the providence of God.

Breathe your Spirit of peace
into our tired, withered souls, O Risen One.
May that peace re-create us in Easter hope,
that we may become your church of peace,
ministers of your forgiveness
and witnesses of your resurrection
to our broken, crucified world.

Third Sunday of Easter

The Risen Jesus appears to his disciples at the Sea of Tiberias. Jesus said to Simon the third time, "Simon, son of John, do you love me?"

John 21: 1–19

The return of the keys

Bobby messed up — big time. Mom and Dad let him take the car Saturday night to take his girlfriend to the movies. Well, things got out of hand. On the way, they picked up a friend and then another friend.... Bobby wasn't paying attention as he should have and ran a red light ... he was stopped by the police ... an open container (not Bobby's) was found in the back seat....

His parents were called. Without a word, Bobby handed over his set of car keys to Mom and Dad — and didn't expect to see them for a long time.

The following Monday, Mom asked Bobby if he could take his grandmother to her doctor's appointment after school. Sure, Bobby said, and Mom gave him the keys. Bobby got Gram to the doctor on time, waited for her, and then took her to do some errands. They both had a great time. Returning home, Bobby handed the keys back to Mom.

A couple of days later, Mom was delayed at work. She called Bobby and asked him to pick up something for dinner. Sure, he said. He took the extra set of keys from the kitchen drawer and headed downtown. Stopping at a light, he saw some of his friends from school. They were on their way to the mall and asked him to go along. No, he said, he had to take care of some stuff. Bobby picked up dinner and got it home. He helped his Mom and sister unpack everything and set the table. Then Bobby returned the keys to the drawer.

On Saturday, Bobby was in his room when his dad came in. Would Bobby take a run to the nursery and pick up some bags of topsoil and mulch? Dad tossed the keys to Bobby and Bobby headed out. He returned an hour later with the material. He then spent the morning helping his dad spread the mulch and plant new shrubs and spring flowers in the yard.

When they both went in for lunch, Bobby handed the keys to his father.

"No," his dad said matter-of-factly, "you hold on to them."

Bobby's Mom and Dad understand that just as they must hold their son accountable for what he had done, they also must give Bobby a chance to restore their trust in him. That's what Jesus does for Peter in today's Gospel.

In asking Peter to profess his love three times, Jesus is not taunting Peter but calling Peter to move beyond the past in order to take on the new challenges of apostleship. In forgiving Peter as he does, in affecting reconciliation with Peter, Jesus transforms Peter's regret and shame into a new understanding and conviction of the Gospel the fisherman has witnessed.

Chapter 21 is a kind of "appendix" to John's Gospel (John 20: 30–31 seems to be the original ending of the Gospel). Jesus' appearance at the Sea of Tiberias recorded in John 21 may have been included to challenge those who doubted the physical resurrection of Jesus, who believed that what the disciples saw were visions or hallucinations. Here the Risen Jesus is a very real and physical presence who points to the fish, lights the fire, cooks and serves the fish.

In a scene reminiscent of Luke 5: 1–11, Peter and a group of apostles have been fishing all night and have caught nothing. At daybreak, Jesus appears on shore and tells them to try casting their net on the starboard side. The catch is a living parable of the Church's apostolic mission: the number 153 is probably intended as a universal number (some have suggested that it represents the number of known species of fish at the time), indicating the Church's mission to all men and women; the unbroken net may also be seen as a symbol of the new Church. The miraculous catch includes two typical Johannine themes: the contrast of light and darkness, day (the resurrection) and night (sin and evil), and the

Eucharistic overtone of the meal, of Jesus taking bread and fish and giving it to Peter and the disciples.

After the meal, sitting by the fire he has made, Jesus invites Peter to atone for his triple denial of Jesus by the fire in the high priest's courtyard by declaring three times his complete love and unfailing devotion to him in the light of this Easter fire. Jesus the Good Shepherd (John 10) passes on the role of servant/shepherd to Peter and his brothers. It is a moment of re-creation and resurrection for Peter.

The Easter Christ calls us to embrace that same model of forgiveness: to possess the greatness of heart to forgive and seek forgiveness; to seek to rebuild and restore trust with those from whom we are estranged, with those we have hurt and who have hurt us, with all who "mess up" — big time.

Christ our Redeemer,
mend our nets and guide our boats,
as we make our way across the oceans of our lives.
May we become your church of reconciliation
  and peace,
the place where no one is beyond your grace
  and redemption.
Help us to overcome our own hurts and anger,
our sense of unworthiness and embarrassment,
in order to be ministers of mercy to one another.

"My sheep hear my voice … "

John 10: 27–30

Final Exam

When Pauline Chen began medical school, she dreamed of saving lives. What she did not count on was how much death would be a part of her work. She chronicles her wrestling with medicine's profound paradox in her book, *Final Exam: A Surgeon's Reflections on Mortality.*

When a patient is dying in the intensive care unit, the protocol is always the same in every hospital: Doors and curtains are closed around the patient and family, monitors are turned off — and physicians make themselves scarce. But one death she witnessed during her internship dramatically changed Doctor Chen's thinking. Early one morning, a patient's heart began to fail after his long battle with colon cancer. Doctor Chen called the family and the attending surgeon. The dying man's wife arrived first. Doctor Chen took her to her husband's room and quietly slipped out, as protocol dictated. But when the attending surgeon arrived, he took the woman's hand and quietly explained what was happening. She began to sob. But then, contrary to the norm, the doctor closed the curtains around the three of them.

Doctor Chen remembers:

"I peeked in. Inside, the woman was still sobbing, but she was standing with her hand in her husband's. The surgeon stood next to her and whispered something; the woman nodded and her sobs subsided. Her shoulders relaxed and her breathing became more regular. The surgeon whispered again, pointing to the monitors and to the patient's chest and then gently putting his hand on the patient's arm. He was, I thought, explaining how life leaves the body — the last contractions of the heart, the irregular breaths, the final comfort of her presence.… Thirty minutes passed before the surgeon stepped out. Soon after, the patient's wife appeared; her husband had died. She thanked us, smiled weakly, and walked out of the ICU."

What the attending surgeon did that morning had a profound effect on Doctor Chen. She stopped slipping away from her dying patients but stayed with them and their families, answering questions, explaining what was happening, offering comfort and consolation.

"From that moment on," Doctor Chen writes, "I would believe that I could do something more than cure."

Christ the Good Shepherd calls us to listen consciously, deliberately, wisely for his voice in the depths of our hearts, to listen for his voice in the love and joy, the pain and anguish, the cries for mercy and justice of those around us; Christ the Son of God assures us that we are always safe and accepted in the loving embrace of his Father. In turn, to be disciples of Christ is to be the voice of Christ and the embrace of God for one another, in the compassion, peace and forgiveness we work for and offer in the Spirit of the Risen One.

Today's brief Gospel is the conclusion of the Good Shepherd discourse in Chapter 10 of John's Gospel. Yahweh, the eternal shepherd of Israel (cf. Ezekiel 34), has raised up his own Son as the Good Shepherd to guide the new Israel of the Church to eternal life. In listening to the voice of Jesus the Good Shepherd, the "flock" finds its way to the Father.

To embrace the true joy of this Easter season is to open our hearts and spirits, our minds and consciousness to hear the voice of God in our midst and then echo that voice in our living the Gospel of the Easter Christ.

Jesus the Good Shepherd,
open our hearts and spirits to hear your voice
amid the noise that surrounds us,
the demands that overwhelm us,
the messages screaming for our attention and action.
May we hear your voice in the cries of others,
see your face in their hurts,
take your hand in the compassion we offer to those
in need.

"This is how all will know that you are my disciples, if you love one another."

John 13: 31–33, 34–35

The secret of Nyamirambo

In 1994, the small East African country of Rwanda was a bloodbath of tribal warfare. More than 800,000 people were killed when the Hutu tribe came to power and began the slaughter of the Tutsi minority.

The one place in the country not touched by the genocide was the small Muslim village of Nyamirambo. A visitor to the village asked his host how Nyamirambo managed not only to avoid the violence but become a refuge to victims. The host explained:

"Because [the villagers'] identity as Muslims is so fundamental, so important to them, that they could not envision killing another. Their commitment to Allah created their fundamental identity, more important than any tribal or national identity."[1]

Love — selfless, complete and unconditional — marks our identity as baptized disciples of the Risen One. Jesus' commandment of "love" is envisioned in the community of Church he leaves behind.

Today's Gospel takes place in the cenacle the night of the Last Supper. Jesus has just completed the dramatic washing of his disciples' feet and has further shocked his disciples with the warnings of Judas' role in the events to come. After Judas leaves, Jesus addresses the remaining eleven — though they do not grasp the full import of what he is saying. An ending is at hand; but also a beginning. Their present friendship is about to be transformed forever into a new community, bound together by the same love that binds Father to Son.

Jesus gives them a "new" commandment of love — what is "new" is the model Jesus leaves them of selfless, sacrificial, forgiving love: a "new" standard of love that transcends legalisms and measurements, that renews and re-creates all human relationships that transforms the most Godless and secular world view into the compassion and justice of God.

As a Church, we come together at the "command" of Christ to accompany one another through our lives' journeys to the reign of God, to support one another in life's joys and sorrows. Our identity as a Church, as disciples of the Risen Christ, is centered in the love that unites the Father and Son and each of us to one another.

Make us the vision of your love, O Lord,
for our own time and place.
May compassion be the light by which we walk;
may the reconciliation be the road we journey;
may humility and selflessness be our guides.
In our own humble efforts
to follow your commandment of love,
may others realize your love for them;
in our struggles to live your Gospel,
may the world recognize your presence in its midst.

Sixth Sunday of Easter

" … the Father will give another Advocate to be with you always, the Spirit of truth, whom the world cannot accept, because it neither sees nor knows him."

John 14: 23–29

Blessed blisters

The newspaper comic strip *Stone Soup* is cartoonist Jan Eliot's take on the modern family as seen through the trials and tribulations of two sisters, Val and Joan, and their families.

One series of strips chronicled 13-year-old Holly's spring-break trip to California. Holly, a teen drama queen of the first order, has been invited by her "cool" Aunt Margie to California for the week. Holly thinks she is going for a week of sun, surfing and shopping — but she arrives to find that she has been "volunteered" by her aunt to work on a "Habitat for Humanity" project. At first, she is furious that she has to spend her week off from school working at a construction site; but during the week she meets the family who will move into the house, including their 13-year-old daughter Gini. Holly is genuinely moved by the family's plight and realizes that she could not have had a better, more fulfilling spring break.

Holly and Aunt Margie spend her last day in California at the beach. The week has had a profound effect on her.

"Aunt Margie? Thanks for inviting us to visit," Holly says.

"I hope you had fun," Aunt Margie says.

"I did! I didn't think I would … but helping a house for charity … I never thought I could do something so … so …"

"Important?" Aunt Margie offers.

Holly looks at her red, chapped hands. "Who knew blisters could feel so good."[2]

Holly discovers the joy that can only be experienced by giving to others, the fulfillment that comes from emptying ourselves of our own wants and putting aside our own needs to help others realize their wants and needs. That is the love of God the Father and Son that Jesus speaks of in today's Gospel; that is how the peace of the Risen Christ is realized in our homes and communities; that is the Spirit, the Advocate/Paraclete leading us and animating us to transform our world.

In his Last Supper discourse, Jesus leaves his fledgling Church his gift of peace and the promise of the Spirit. Peace that is of Christ is not just the absence of violence or conflict, but a deep sense of love, justice, truth and mercy, an understanding of our connectedness to one another as children of the same God that are the principal motivations of our actions, behavior and values. Gospel peace is not passive; it calls for an active response from us: to work to break through the barriers which divide us, to learn to understand one another and to pardon those who hurt us. Christ's peace is that sense within us that compels us to spend our spring breaks building Habitat Houses; that inspires us to volunteer for one of our parish's many ministries of compassion and support to children, family, the poor, the elderly; that gives us the grace and courage to stand up and sacrifice for what is right and just in our communities and nation.

The "Advocate" (or "Paraclete," as translated in some versions of John's Gospel), who intercedes and intervenes on behalf of good, is the exact opposite of the "adversary," Satan. The Advocate/Paraclete is that presence of God within us that opens our hearts and minds to the promptings of God's Word as proclaimed by Jesus.

In sacrament, in Scripture, in community, in our living of the Gospel in our every day lives, the Risen Christ is in our midst. In even our smallest act of selfless kindness — prompted by the Paraclete instructing our open hearts and spirit — we reveal the presence of the Easter Christ in our little piece of the world. Like Holly, may we discover the Christ-like joy of "blisters" suffered in the pursuit of bringing the love of God into our homes and hearts.

Send your Spirit upon us, O God,
that we may realize the joy of being
your sons and daughters.
Come make your dwelling in us,
that we may become vessels of your grace and peace
for all homes and hearts.
Plant the seed of your Word within us,
that we may become branches of your compassion
in the most barren places.
May the Advocate make us,
in our own time and place,
teachers of your just Word,
prophets of your coming reign,
witnesses of your compassion and grace
in this life and in the life to come.

Ascension of the Lord

" ... you will receive power when the Holy Spirit comes upon you, and you will be my witnesses in Jerusalem, throughout Judea and Samaria, and to the ends of the earth." When Jesus had said this, as they were looking on, Jesus was lifted up, and a cloud took him from their sight.

Acts 1:1–11

"You are witnesses of these things."

Luke 24: 46–53

The "God words"

A pastor remembers a special parishioner:

Electra was four years old and lived with her mother in a welfare hotel. At a Thanksgiving dinner for the homeless, the pastor invited them to stay with his family for the weekend. Little Electra noticed that her new friends prayed before meals. Electra implored them, "Please, teach me the God words." The little girl committed the simple words of the table blessing to memory.

When they returned home, Electra taught the words to her neighbors in the hotel. Her mother later told the pastor that the child could no longer bite into a peanut butter sandwich without making everyone around her say "the God words."[3]

On the Mount of the Ascension, Jesus commissions his small band of followers to teach "the God words." Today's readings include two accounts of that moment by the same writer:

Reading 1 is the beginning of the Acts of the Apostles, Luke's "Gospel of the Holy Spirit." Jesus' Ascension begins volume two of Luke's work. The words and images here evoke the First Covenant accounts of the ascension of Elijah (2 Kings 2) and the forty years of the Exodus: Luke considers the time that the Risen Lord spent with his disciples a sacred time, a "desert experience" for the apostles to prepare them for their new ministry of preaching the Gospel of the Resurrection. Responding to their question about the restoration of Israel, Jesus discourages his disciples from guessing what cannot be known. Greater things await them as his "witnesses." In the missionary work awaiting them, Christ will be with them in the presence of the promised Spirit.

Whereas in Acts Luke places Jesus' Ascension 40 days after Easter, in his Gospel the Ascension takes place on Easter night. Luke treats the same event from two points of view: in the Gospel, the Ascension is the completion of Jesus' Messianic work; in Acts, it is the prelude to the Church's mission.

The words Jesus addresses to his disciples on the mountain of the Ascension are addressed to all of us two millennia later. We are called to teach, to witness and to heal in our own small corners of the world, to hand on to others the story that has been handed on to us about Jesus and his Gospel of love and compassion.

We have experienced the extraordinary event of Christ in our lives — now Christ hands on to us the responsibility of bringing the blessings and grace of that experience to others. The Jesus of the Ascension commissions us to share the "God words" with those who have not heard them, to bring the "palm branches" of Christ's victory to the hurting and forgotten in our midst.

Risen Lord,
make us witnesses of your resurrection.
May your constant presence
in the midst of your Church
be a wellspring of grace
and the light that illuminates our work
as we struggle to proclaim your reign
of justice and mercy
here, in this time, and in the time to come.

[In some churches and dioceses, the Ascension of the Lord is celebrated on the Seventh Sunday of Easter.]

"Father, I pray … for those who will believe in me through their word, so that all may be one, as you, Father, are in me and I in you … "

John 17: 20–26

Final prayers

Late morning is Amelia's favorite time of the day. The Hospice volunteers have helped her get washed and dressed. After preparing her breakfast, they go quietly about whatever household tasks need to be done. That gives Amelia this quiet time in her sunroom.

Amelia is at peace. She is grateful for the days — though numbered — that she has left. In this quiet time every morning, she fingers her rosary, but the photographs of her family that cover the table near her rocker are her real prayer beads. She picks each one up gently. She prays that her son will do well in his new job … that her daughter continues to conquer the challenges of her medical career … that her grandson will choose the right college and grow into adulthood … that her granddaughter will be born whole and healthy.

"Hold them all, O Lord, in your hand," Amelia prays. "Bless them as you have blessed my husband and me these many years."

In John's account of the Last Supper, after his final teachings to his disciples before the events of his passion begin, Jesus addresses his Father in heaven. He begins praying for himself, that he may obediently bring to completion the work of redemption entrusted to him by the Father. Next he prays for his disciples, that they may faithfully proclaim the word he has taught them. Finally (today's Gospel), Jesus prays for the future Church — us — that we may be united in the "complete" love that binds the Father to the Son and the Son to his Church, and that in our love for one another the world may come to know God.

The same anxieties and hopes that Amelia voices in her prayers for those she loves and is about to leave behind Jesus voices in his prayers. In this touching scene from John's account of the Last Supper, we see and hear Jesus commending every disciple of every time and place — and that includes all of us — to his Father. In his "high priestly prayer," we behold our connectedness to the Church of all times and places: from the Risen Christ's greeting of peace Easter night to our own *Alleluias* this Easter. The night before he dies, Jesus prays that we realize his hope for his Church: a Church of welcome and acceptance that seeks to find and honor what unites and binds us together as the people of God.

As Amelia gathers her family in prayer, may we gather one another, always and everywhere, into prayer before the God to whom we all belong, the God who gives us all things in Christ.

Christ Jesus, Risen Lord and High Priest,
make us sharers in the work of building your Church.
Make us one in the love that binds you to the Father.
Make us complete in the sacred dignity
that everyone of us possesses as children of the Father
and brothers and sisters in and of you.

Pentecost

All of them were filled with the Holy Spirit and began to speak in other languages, as the Spirit gave them ability.
Acts 2: 1–11

Jesus breathed on them and said: "Receive the Holy Spirit … "
John 20: 19–23

God's instrument

It begins as a piece of hollowed wood or metal tubing. Then a craftsman, using skills and tools that have been passed down for centuries, meticulously shapes the wood and metal, carefully drills holes in the shaft, devises a system of stops and valves in the metal, installs an intricate system of strings, tuning keys and hammers. The wood is then beautifully finished with resins and varnish; the metal is polished until it gleams. The craftsman's long hours of detailed work results in a finished flute or violin or guitar or piano.

But the completed instrument, though a beautiful work of art, remains just a piece of wood or metal until a musician takes it up and breathes into it while gliding his or her fingers across the stops or carefully manipulates the strings and keys. Then that piece of hollowed wood, that tube of metal, is transformed into a musical instrument, a portal for us to a world of beauty and transcendence.

The mystery of the Church is like a musical instrument. God has formed us into a community, an instrument for bringing his life and love into our world. But what makes our Church more than just a gathering of good people is God's "breath" infusing the Church with the music of his divinity. The feast of Pentecost celebrates that unseen, immeasurable presence of God in our lives and in our Church — the *ruah* that animates us to do the work of Gospel justice and mercy, the *ruah* that makes God's will our will, the *ruah* of God living in us and transforming us so that we might bring his life and love to our broken world. God "breathes" his Spirit into our souls that we may live in his life and love; God ignites the "fire" of his Spirit within our hearts and minds that we may seek God in all things in order to realize the coming of his reign.

Pentecost was the Jewish festival of the harvest (also called the Feast of Weeks), celebrated 50 days after Passover, when the first fruits of the corn harvest were offered to the Lord. A feast of pilgrimage (hence the presence in Jerusalem of so many "devout Jews of every nation"), Pentecost also commemorated Moses' receiving the Law on Mount Sinai. For the new Israel, Pentecost becomes the celebration of the Spirit of God's compassion, peace and forgiveness — the Spirit that transcends the Law and becomes the point of departure for the young Church's universal mission.

In his Acts of the Apostles (Reading 1), Luke evokes the Old Testament images of wind and fire in his account of the new Church's Pentecost: God frequently revealed his presence in fire (the pillar of fire in the Sinai) and in wind (the wind that sweeps over the earth to make the waters of the Great Flood subside). The Hebrew word for spirit, *ruah*, and the Greek word *pneuma* also refer to the movement of air, not only as wind, but also of life-giving breath (as in God's creation of man in Genesis 2 and the revivification of the dry bones in Ezekiel 37). Through his life-giving "breath," the Lord begins the era of the new Israel on Pentecost.

Today's Gospel of the first appearance of the Risen Jesus before his ten disciples (remember Thomas is not present) on Easter night is John's version of the Pentecost event. In "breathing" the Holy Spirit upon them, Jesus imitates God's act of creation in Genesis. Just as Adam's life came from God, so the disciples' new life of the Spirit comes from Jesus. In the Resurrection, the Spirit replaces their sense of self-centered fear and confusion with the "peace" of understanding, enthusiasm and joy and shatters all barriers among them to make of them a community of hope and forgiveness. By Christ's sending them forth, the disciples become *apostles* — "those sent."

In Jesus' breathing upon the assembled disciples on Easter night the new life of the Spirit, the community of the Resurrection — the Church — takes flight. That same Spirit continues to "blow" through our experience of Church to give life and direction to our mission and ministry to preach the Gospel to every nation, to proclaim forgiveness and reconciliation in God's name, to immerse all of humanity into the life and love of God manifested in Jesus' Resurrection.

Come, Spirit of God.
and breathe your *ruah* through your Church.
Animate us to love as you have loved us.
Inspire us to follow your example
  of humble and gracious servanthood.
Compel us to seek your justice and mercy in all things.
Come, Holy Spirit,
re-create us in the peace of the Risen One,
that may become Christ's vision
of a Church of compassion and forgiveness.

Solemnities of the Lord in Ordinary Time

The Holy Trinity

" ... The Spirit of truth ... will guide you to all truth. Everything that the Father has is mine; for this reason I told you that he will take from what is mine and declare it to you."

John 16: 12–15

"Once upon a time ..."

A writer has an idea for a book. He or she nurses it along in his or her mind, organizing it, refining it, finding the precise words to articulate it.

After many long hours of hard work, the idea becomes a book, and the idea can now be touched, seen and heard. As a book, the idea generates energy — an energy that affects all who read it, maybe even changing the lives of its readers. And while some may like the book, others may dislike it so much they will do their best to destroy it, by bad reviews, whispering campaigns, or burning it in the public square. In spite of the attempts to destroy the book, those who have been inspired and moved by the work draw ongoing power from it, sharing its message with others. Some will remember parts of the book; some will write down everything they can remember of the book; and some will tell all who will listen the wonderful story or facts contained in the book. The power released by the book endures long after its pages are no more.

Dorothy Sayers, in an essay in *The Mind of the Maker,* offers this image for contemplating the mystery of God. God is the writer with the idea — an idea for a world of men and women created in his image who live in his love. The idea takes the form of a "book" — Jesus, the human "face" of that idea. Despite the failed attempts of some to destroy the book, the energy of the book endures: the book takes on a power that "rises" above those who seek to "crucify" the idea. Such is the Spirit of God giving life to the idea and inspiring those who embrace it.

Idea, word, power — the God of the Trinity.

Today's celebration of the Trinity (originating in France in the eighth century and adopted by the universal Church in 1334) focuses on the essence of our faith: the revelation of God as Creator, the climax of his creation in Jesus the Redeemer, the fullness of the love of God poured out upon us in the Sustainer Spirit.

In his final words to his disciples at the Last Supper, Jesus promises to send the "Spirit of truth [to] guide you to all truth." The Son has revealed the Father to the Church; the Spirit of truth and wisdom keeps that revelation alive in the Church.

Trinity Sunday is a celebration of the many ways in which we discover the *why* of God: God, the Creator and Sustainer of all that lives; God, the Christ who became one of us to show us the depth of God's love; the Spirit, the love of God living among us, the love that gives meaning and vision to us, God's beloved creation.

Faith begins with realizing the Spirit of God breathing life into all that exists; faith then compels us to continue the creative work of God, to embrace and be embraced by the love of God that envelopes every wonder of nature and every manifestation of compassion. Discerning truth, likewise, is an ongoing process; God continues to reveal himself in all time. He is not a silent God who ceased to reveal himself on the last page of Scripture. Through the Spirit dwelling within us and within the Church, God is still leading us into a greater realization of what Jesus taught in the Gospels.

To be a person of authentic faith means to seek out and face the truth — regardless of the consequences, regardless of the cost to egos or wallets, regardless of our doubts and cynicism and fear. To live our faith means to live the truth about love, justice and forgiveness with integrity and conviction, regardless of the cost.

May we embrace God's "idea" of love and reconciliation as mirrored in the "book" of the Gospel Jesus; may that idea energize us to transform our world in that idea through the power of the ever-present Spirit.

May we behold your presence, O God,
in all its wonders and grace,
in every moment of our lives.
May everything we do give praise to you
as Father:
  the loving Creator and Sustainer of all life;
as Son:
  the Word and Light of God made human for us;
as Spirit:
  the love that binds Father to Son,
  and we to you and to one another.

Then taking the five loaves and two fish, and looking up to heaven, Jesus said the blessing over them, broke them, and gave them to the disciples to set before the crowd.

Luke 9: 11–17

The four verbs

She had just retired after 40 years in the classroom. After a year of traveling, gardening and reading, she found that she missed the kids. So she volunteered to tutor a couple of afternoons a week. One student was having a particularly hard time with equations. So she made some time available to work with the student after school and, together, they struggled through the mystery of mathematics. Nothing made her happier when the student received an "A' on his next math test.

After graduation, he became a missionary priest, working in a poor barrio in the Philippines. He would often write to his friends back home, telling them about the wonderful people in his parish and their struggles. His friends, in turn, set up a fund for their friend and organized fundraisers to build a new well for his parish, stock the clinic and school with supplies and take care of repairs on the mission's buildings. He is grateful for their help; his friends are honored to be part of such holy work.

Every summer the counselors stay a few extra days for the annual "Special Kids' Camp." After a long summer working at the nonprofit camp and before returning to school, many of the college students happily give their time to provide a camping experience for kids with cancer, kids confined to wheelchairs, kids with all kinds of mental and physical challenges. It is the best summer of their lives. It's a demanding weekend and, come Sunday, the counselors are exhausted — but they will be the first to tell you that it's the best part of their summer.

The retired teacher, the friends of a missioner and the counselors all imitate the actions of Jesus in today's Gospel: they *take* from what they have, they *"bless"* it by the God-like compassion in which they will give it, they *break* it from their own need and want, and *give* it to another. Their generous act becomes a sacrament — the manifestation of God's love in our midst.

The feeding of the crowd with five loaves of bread and two fish — the only one of Jesus' miracles recounted in all four Gospels — was especially cherished by the early Church. They saw Jesus' feeding of the multitude as a precursor to the Eucharistic banquet that would bind them — and binds us — into the Church of the Risen One. Luke will use these same four verbs — *take, bless, break, give* — to describe Jesus' institution of the Eucharist at the Last Supper (Luke 22: 17–20).

But we, too, can perform wonders in our own time and place by imitating those four decisive Eucharistic verbs: *take, bless, break, give* — *taking* from what we have, *blessing* it by offering it to others in the spirit of God's love, *breaking* it from our own needs and interests for the sake of others, and *giving* it with joy-filled gratitude to the God who has blessed us with so much. In acting on the four verbs of the Eucharist in our everyday lives, we become what we receive in the sacrament of the body and blood of the Lord.

As you give to us, O God, may we give to one another.
May our humble acts of compassion, generosity
  and forgiveness
become visible signs of your invisible grace.
As Christ takes, blesses, breaks and gives his body to us
  in the Eucharist,
may we take, bless, break and give from our own need
  to become Eucharist for others.

ORDINARY TIME

NOTE: The Sundays in this section are numbered according to both the Roman lectionary's designation of Sundays of the Year (Ordinary Time) and the Common lectionary's designation of Sundays after the Epiphany and Propers (Sundays after Pentecost).

Second Sunday of the Year / Second Sunday after the Epiphany

At a wedding feast in Cana, Jesus told them, "Fill the jars with water … Draw some out now and take it to the headwaiter."

John 2: 1–11

Re-dreaming

A young woman is set up on a blind date with a young pediatrician. He is painfully shy and awkward; stumbling to keep up a coherent conversation with her, he spills soup on his tie during dinner. As the woman is contemplating faking a headache and asking to be taken home early, the doctor's beeper goes off. He is called to an emergency and invites her to come along, since it was on the way to her home. Seeing him interact with a sick child, she discovers a tenderness in him that surprises her and she begins to speculate about what sort of husband and father he might be. If he isn't that man of her dreams, she wonders, maybe it's time for her to change those dreams.[1]

New dreams begin to be realized as we begin the story of Jesus.

Today's Gospel is John's account of Jesus' first great "sign": the transformation of water into wine at the wedding feast at Cana. For the churches of the East, the miracle at Cana is the fourth great event of the Lord's Epiphany or manifestation to the world (the first three: his birth at Bethlehem, the adoration of the magi, and his baptism at the Jordan by John). Despite Jesus' protestations to his mother, his time as Messiah is now upon the world (at least Mary has no doubt).

Cana brings together two important Scriptural symbols that point to the Messiahship of Jesus:

Wine in abundance was considered a sign of the Messianic age to come (one example: Isaiah 54: 5–14, Reading 4 for the Easter Vigil). The water in the six large stone jars used for the ritual washings prescribed by the first covenant law is transformed by Jesus into wine, prefiguring the new covenant to be sealed in Jesus' blood (which we celebrate in the wine of the Eucharist).

The limitless love of God for his people is exalted throughout Scripture in the image of *marriage.* Today's first reading from Isaiah (62: 1–5) is a beautiful example of this tradition; in the Gospels, Jesus refers to himself as "the Bridegroom" who comes to bring his people to the wedding feast of the Father. The love between spouses is the strongest (if still imperfect) image we have to understand the depth of God's love for his holy people.

The evangelist John pulls together these two powerful Messianic symbols of wine and marriage to introduce the public ministry of Jesus, the long-awaited Messiah. Cana is the first sign that God has begun something new in the midst of his "Delight" and "Espoused." God's time has come to dream new dreams — hope that transforms hurt into reconciliation, despair into confidence, alienation into community.

Compassionate God,
may we dare to hope in your mercy and compassion.
Let your grace and wisdom enlighten our vision
and open our hearts
to dream your dream of justice and reconciliation
for all your sons and daughters.
In imitating Christ the Bridegroom's humble service,
may we press "new wine" for our common tables;
in our love and compassion for one another,
may all of our brothers and sisters find their places
at your Son's wedding feast.

Third Sunday of the Year / Third Sunday after the Epiphany

Jesus unrolled the scroll and found the message where it was written: "The Spirit of the LORD is upon me ..." Jesus said to them, "Today this Scripture passage is fulfilled in your hearing."

Luke 1: 1–4; 4: 14–21

"We do cancer ..."

Richard was a widower; his wife had suffered a long and painful death from cancer. Then he met Celia; they came to love each other and each other's children dearly.

Less than a year into their courtship, Celia discovered a lump in her breast. She had gone to the doctor by herself and was alone when she received the devastating news: the lump was malignant.

Almost her first thought was of Richard and his children. They had been profoundly wounded by his wife's and their mother's cancer only a few years before and were still healing from it. How could she bring this terrible thing into their lives again?

She called Richard immediately and, without telling him why, simply broke off their relationship. For several weeks she refused his phone calls and returned his letters. But Richard would not give up and begged her to see him.

Finally, Celia relented and arranged to meet him to say good-bye. When they met, she could see the deep strain and hurt on his face. Richard gently asked Celia why she had broken up with him. Finally, on the verge of tears, she told Richard the truth: that she had found a lump in her breast, that it was malignant, that she had undergone surgery a few weeks before and would begin chemotherapy the following week.

"You and the children have lived through this once already," she told him. "I won't put you through it again."

He looked at her, his jaw dropping. "You have cancer?" he asked. Dumbly, she nodded, the tears beginning to run down her cheeks.

"Oh, Celia," he said — and began to laugh with relief. "We can *do* cancer … we know how to *do* cancer. I thought that you didn't love me."

Oh, but she did. And they got through it together, happily married.[2]

Richard, who has dealt with the cancer of a loved one, becomes the fulfillment of Isaiah's hope for Celia. He and his children will mirror for her the "glad tidings" Jesus has come to proclaim.

In Luke's Gospel, Jesus begins his teaching ministry in Galilee. Galilee — a name which comes from the Hebrew word for *circle* — was a great agricultural region encircled by non-Jewish nations and cultures, thereby earning Galilee a reputation for being the most progressive and least conservative area of Palestine. A teacher with a "new" message such as this Rabbi Jesus would be expected to receive a favorable hearing in the openness of Galilean society.

Jesus returns to his hometown (after his forty-day desert retreat — the Gospel for the First Sunday of Lent), to the Galilean city of Nazareth. Nazareth was a city of great importance in Israel's history and economy, located on the major routes to Jerusalem, Alexandria and Damascus. In the Nazareth synagogue (where Jewish communities outside of Jerusalem would gather for teaching and prayer), Jesus announces, using the words of the prophet Isaiah, the fulfillment of God's promise of a Messiah for Israel.

As witnesses of Christ's resurrection, as baptized disciples of his Gospel, we inherit the Spirit's call to "bring glad tidings" and "proclaim the Lord's favor" to the poor, the imprisoned, the blind, the oppressed and the helpless. Whatever gifts and graces we possess can work great and wondrous things when done in the Spirit of God. Whether we can "do cancer," whether we know how to comfort and console another, whether we can make a soup kitchen or a tutoring program work, we make Isaiah's vision a reality in our own Nazareths.

In the Roman lectionary, today's Gospel reading begins with the brief prologue to Luke's Gospel (Luke 1: 1–4). Luke begins his Gospel in the classic Greek historical style by personally (Luke is the only one of the four evangelists who ever refers to himself in the first person) assuring his readers (addressed to the person of "Theophilus," Greek for friend of God) of the historical accuracy and theological authenticity of the story he is about to chronicle. Luke has assembled his account from various fragments and stories told and retold for the nascent Christian movement.

Luke, the author of this year's cycle of Gospel readings, is a "second generation" Christian. Greek by birth and a physician by profession, he is believed to have been a traveling companion of Paul, through whom he met Mark and perhaps Peter himself. Though not an eyewitness to the Gospel he has compiled, Luke knows the Jewish Scriptures. He writes his Gospel mainly for Gentiles like himself: for Luke, this Jesus fulfills not only Jewish dreams but every people's hopes for wholeness and holiness.

Luke's Gospel reflects a scientist's precision in locating dates, places and people; but Luke's Gospel also exhibits an interest in people rather than ideas. His account celebrates the compassion of Jesus for the outcasts and "second class citizens" of Jewish society, especially women. Luke's story of this Jesus who comes to "proclaim glad tidings to the poor … to announce a year of favor from the Lord" should make a profound difference in the lives of all who hear it. In his humanity, Luke's Jesus reveals a God who is approachable and present to us in all that is good and right and loving around us.

May your Spirit come upon us, O God,
that we may help others rejoice in your presence
in all our lives,
that we may bring hope and healing
to broken relationships and old hurts,
that we may be freed from the distractions and detours
that impede our search for you,
that we may seek your reconciliation and forgiveness
in this blessed time you have given us.

Fourth Sunday of the Year / Fourth Sunday after the Epiphany

"Amen, I say to you, no prophet is accepted in his own native place."

Luke 4: 21–30

The Sign of Jonah

Shortly after World War II, a Lutheran minister named Gunter Rutenborn wrote and staged a play he titled *The Sign of Jonah* that had profound impact on the city of Berlin.

The play takes place in a Germany still reeling from the war. The play begins with a group of refugees trying to determine who is to blame for this horror. Some blame Hitler, of course; others indict the munitions manufacturers who financed Hitler; still others claim the German people themselves bear responsibility for the destruction of their country.

Suddenly, a man in the crowd speaks up: "Do you want to know who is really to blame for all the suffering we've been through? I'll tell you. God is to blame. He created this world. He placed all of this power in such unworthy hands. He allowed all of this to happen."

At first, everyone is taken back by the accusation, but gradually the chorus is picked up by all: *God is to blame! God is to blame!*

And so God is brought down on stage and put on trial for the crime of creation — and He is found guilty. The judge then pronounces sentence: "The crime is so severe that it demands the worst possible sentences. I hereby sentence God to live on this earth as a human being."

Three archangels are called down to execute the sentence.

The first angel declares, "I'm going to see to it that when God serves his sentence, He knows what it is like to be obscure and poor. He will be born in a ghetto. There will be shame about his birth. And he will live as a Jew."

The second angel vows, "I'm going to see to it that when God serves his sentence he knows what it is like to fail and suffer disappointment. No one will understand what He is trying to do; he will be cursed and humiliated despite the good He does."

The third angel swears, "I'm going to see to it that when God serves his sentence, He will learn what it is to suffer physical pain. He will die the most painful and humiliating death imaginable."

And the play ends with the three angels disappearing to carry out the sentence.

And so, God's "sentence" is carried out in the Gospel accounts of Jesus, God-made-human. The second angel's vow begins to be fulfilled in today's Lucan pericope, the beginning of Jesus' public ministry.

Today's Gospel continues last Sunday's account of Jesus' teaching in the synagogue at Nazareth. After proclaiming the fulfillment of Isaiah's vision of the Messiah (last Sunday's Gospel), Jesus sits down — the posture assumed by one who is about to teach — and begins by explaining in no uncertain terms that he cannot perform any healings or miracles there because of their lack of faith. He teaches that the Messiah does not come for Nazareth alone but for every people and nation of every place and age.

His explanation is met with indignation and anger. Many Jews of the time were so convinced that they alone were God's own "chosen" people that they despised everyone else. They could not accept Jesus' idea that others — Gentiles! — were as loved by God as they were. Amid such controversy, Jesus is forced to leave his hometown. He begins to pay the price exacted from all "prophets" who stand for what is right, who speak for what is just.

The audiences who saw *The Sign of Jonah* and we who have encountered the Jesus of the Gospels understand immediately that God has completed his sentence. God knows what it is to live as a human being — which means that nothing we face today is alien or unknown to God. The central message of the Gospel Jesus is that God became what we are so that we can better understand what God is and what God is about: love, forgiveness, selflessness. Such is the "good news" of Jesus who enters human history and sanctifies our humanity for all time.

Out of love for us, O God,
you took on our humanity in the person of Jesus
so that we may learn to live our lives
as the very reflection of your holiness.
Only by your grace can we begin to grasp
the mystery of such love.
However imperfectly our attempts,
despite the poverty of our efforts,
let your Spirit open our hearts
to love as you have loved us,
to behold your presence in every act
of compassion and forgiveness,
to speak your words of justice and peace
to our broken world.

Fifth Sunday of the Year /
Fifth Sunday after the Epiphany

After he had finished speaking to the crowds from Simon's boat, Jesus said to Simon, "Put out into deep water and lower your nets for a catch … Do not be afraid; from now on you will be catching men."

Luke 5: 1–11

Sometimes your parents can surprise you …

The teenager had her driver's license for only a few weeks. After much pleading, Dad relented and let her use the family's new car to take her friends to the beach.

She was very careful. She kept under the speed limit all the way. She took great pains to park the car in a safe spot.

But on the trip home, *Crunch*! She never saw the other car. In an instant, the front grill, headlight and part of the door were reduced to a crumbled mass of metal.

She wanted to die. Dad would have her head. *Might as well burn my driver's license*, she thought. *I'll probably be grounded until I'm thirty.*

And so she limped home in her father's once beautiful car, terrified at what awaited her.

As she pulled into the driveway, her parents came running from the house. From the looks on their faces, she knew this would not be a happy homecoming. Dad ran ahead of Mom — right passed the damaged car and pulled her out of the car.

"Dad, I'm sorry — " she stammered.

But he wouldn't let her finish.

"Are you all right? Were you hurt? Was anybody hurt?" he wanted to know, hugging her tighter and tighter.

She began to cry — a little surprised that her Dad was so understanding, and a little ashamed that she had expected so little from him.

It has happened to all of us — just when we expected to pay a heavy price for what we've done or haven't done, parents, spouses and friends react with understanding, compassion and immediate forgiveness. Peter has a similar experience in today's Gospel when he underestimates God's capacity to lift up, to call forth, to inspire.

Luke makes Peter the center of his account of the miraculous catch (while John places this event after the resurrection, Luke makes it part of the call of Simon Peter and the apostles). Peter and his brothers knew that the best time to fish on the Gennesaret (another name for the Sea of Galilee) was at night; little is caught during the heat of the day. So Peter's agreeing to lower his nets at Jesus' urging was, for a fisherman of Peter's savvy and expertise, an act of considerable faith. Jesus' word results in a stunning catch.

Peter's reaction, though surprising, is understandable. It is clear to him who this Jesus is — and his instinctive reaction is to back away. Peter recognizes his own unworthiness and humbleness in the sight of God. But Jesus assures him he has not come to drive sinners from his presence but to bring them back to God — to catch them in the "net" of God's love.

Like Peter, we often expect too little from our relationship with God; many of us suffer from an inferiority complex when it comes to God: we're neither good enough nor wise enough in church protocol to consider ourselves "religious." We cannot imagine, as Peter cannot imagine, God loving sinful, Godless us. But that is the "mystery" of God: that God loves despite ourselves.

Thomas Merton observed that "the root of Christian love is not the will to love but the faith that one is loved by God … irrespective of one's worth. In the true Christian vision of God's love, the idea of worthiness loses significance. The revelation of the mercy of God makes the problem of worthiness something almost laughable … no one could ever, alone, be strictly worthy to be loved with such a love — [such a realization] is a true liberation of spirit."

Assured of God's love for us, we are challenged by Jesus to lower our nets into the "deep water": to risk our own security and comfort for the sake of the Gospel values of compassion, justice and reconciliation. To be a "catcher" of souls requires enough love to extend ourselves to reach out to another and enough faith in God's grace to make the "catch."

Help us to realize, O God,
that you love us, despite ourselves.
May that assurance allay our fears
to put out into deep water
to discover your grace on the seas we sail.
Do not let us hesitate to lower our own nets —
to mirror your love and compassion
in our small, seemingly insignificant acts of generosity,
justice and reconciliation.

Sixth Sunday of the Year / Sixth Sunday after the Epiphany

"Blessed are you who are poor ... but woe to you who are rich ... "

Luke 6: 17, 20–26

Frozen in time

Once in the depth of winter, recounts an Eastern parable, a bird of prey was scouring the frozen landscape for food. On a large ice floe in the river, the bird saw the remains of a deer left behind by hunters. The bird swooped down and began to feast. So consumed by what it was consuming, the bird ignored the sound of water thundering in the distance — a roar that was becoming increasingly louder by the moment. In a matter of seconds the ice floe was just about to go crashing over the river's falls. The bird immediately flapped its wings to escape, but its claws had frozen into the icy remains of the deer. The bird was trapped, powerless to escape.

Like the doomed bird on the ice floe, we become so consumed by amassing the things that mark success that we lose ourselves in the process. In today's Gospel, Jesus spares no words in challenging us to embrace a new attitude and vision as to what separates the rich and poor.

While Jesus speaks of "Beatitudes" in Matthew's Sermon on the Mount, in Luke's Sermon on the Plain, Jesus drops a series of bombshells. He takes the accepted standards of the times and turns them upside down: To those who are considered the "haves" of society, Jesus warns "Woe to you!" — wealth and power are not the stuff of the kingdom of God; but to the "have nots," Jesus says, "Happy and blessed are you" — love, humble selflessness, compassion and generosity are the treasure of God's realm. Jesus promises his followers poverty, suffering, persecution and grief — but their hope in God will be rewarded with perfect and complete joy. The "blessedness" of the poor and forgotten and the treasure of compassion and mercy will be continuing themes in Luke's Gospel (a theme the evangelist introduces in Mary's Canticle, Luke 1: 46–55).

Both as a lesson in living and as a prophecy of the despair brought on by hard economic times, Jesus' teaching in today's Gospel is (excuse the pun) right on the money. We can become so focused on obtaining the good things of life that we devalue the riches we already possess: the love of family and friends, the gift of good health, that special sense of joy we experience when we give of ourselves to others.

Mother Teresa of Calcutta often said that Western Christians suffered from a much deeper and pathetic poverty than her people endured in the slums and ghettos where she and her sisters worked: "The spiritual poverty of the West is much greater than the spiritual poverty of the East. In the West, there are millions of people who suffer loneliness and emptiness, who feel unloved and unwanted. They are not hungry in the physical sense; what is missing is a relationship with God and with each other."

Luke's version of the Beatitudes challenges everything our consumer-oriented society holds dear. While wealth, power and celebrity are the sought-after prizes of our world, the treasures of God's reign are love, humility, compassion and generosity. In freeing ourselves from the pursuit of the things of this world, we liberate ourselves to seek the lasting things of God.

Father, may your Spirit of love and compassion
open our hearts and illuminate our vision
so that we may seek the poverty of love
over the amassing of things;
that we may be rich in the love of family and friends
rather than in the numbers of a paper fortune;
that we may seek places in the eternity of your reign
rather than celebrity in this fleeting moment.

Seventh Sunday of the Year /
Seventh Sunday after the Epiphany

"Love your enemies and do good to them, and lend them expecting nothing back; then your reward will be great ... Forgive and you will be forgiven. Give and gifts will be given to you ... "

Luke 6: 27–38

Lincoln the reconciler

When Abraham Lincoln began his Presidency in 1861, one of his harshest and most bitter opponents was Edwin McMasters Stanton.

Stanton despised Lincoln. A former member of President Buchanan's cabinet, Stanton was unsparing in his criticism of "the imbecility of this administration." In one speech, Stanton called the Illinois lawyer "the original gorilla" and said that the famed explorer of the day Paul De Chaillu was a fool to travel to Africa to study a gorilla when he could have found one so easily in Springfield.

One year into his Presidency, Lincoln was forced to replace the Secretary of War. To the shock of his advisors, Lincoln named Stanton to the critical War post. Despite his harsh criticism of the President, Lincoln considered Stanton a brilliant civil and constitutional lawyer. Though his inner circle pleaded with him to reconsider, Lincoln was firm: "Yes, I know Mr. Stanton. I know all the terrible things he has said about me. But I believe he is the best man for the job."

So Edwin Stanton became Lincoln's Secretary of War. Stanton distinguished himself by his honest and efficient management of departmental affairs and an aggressive prosecution of the Union's war effort.

Three years later, with the end of the Civil War in sight, Abraham Lincoln was assassinated on Good Friday night in Ford's Theater. Upon learning the news, Stanton rushed to the President's side and was with him at his death. Stanton said of the man he once ridiculed, "There lies the greatest ruler of men the world has ever seen. He now belongs to the ages."

In today's Gospel, Jesus exhorts his followers to take a similar approach to the tension and distrust that mars many of our relationships. Continuing his Sermon on the Plain, Jesus turns upside down another accepted standard of Jewish morality. The principle of "do to no one what you yourself dislike" (as articulated in Tobit 4: 15) was not enough for those who seek to be God's holy people. Jesus demands that his disciples "love your enemies." The Greek word for love used in this text is *agape*, a sense of benevolence, kindness and charity towards others — in other words, no matter what a person does to us we will never allow ourselves to seek anything but the highest good for him or her. In every relationship, in every set of circumstances, the faithful disciple of Jesus seeks to break the cycle of hatred and distrust by taking that formidable first step to love and seek reconciliation above all else. The completeness and limitlessness of God's own love and mercy for us should be the measure of our love and mercy for one another.

Lincoln's acknowledgment of Stanton's talents transformed a critic's mistrust and hatred into trust and understanding. St. Augustine preached that "there is no greater invitation to love than loving first." The faithful disciple of Jesus seeks to break that destructive rut of hatred and distrust by putting love and reconciliation above vengeance and restitution.

God of mercy and reconciliation,
make us a people of *agape:*
May we never hesitate to forgive
and seek forgiveness from one another.
May we never let hatred, distrust and hurt

isolate us behind walls of self-righteousness
and anger.
May we take to heart your call to be your ministers
of reconciliation
and your messengers of peace
to our families, parishes and communities.

"Why do you notice the splinter in your brother's eye, but do not perceive the wooden beam in your own … ? For every tree is known by its fruit … A good person out of the store of goodness in his heart produces good …"

Luke 6: 39–45

Assume the position, Christian

A woman stops behind another car at a traffic light. The light turns green, but the driver in the car ahead of her is on his cell phone and doesn't notice the light change. The woman, who is running late, begins pounding her steering wheel and screaming at the man to go. The man still doesn't move. The woman is now raving at the obtuseness of the man. The light turns yellow. The woman blasts her horn; she screams a litany of obscenities and makes a certain unmistakable "gesture" at the man. The man finally looks up, sees the yellow light, and accelerates through the intersection — just as the light turns red again.

The woman, left at the intersection, is beside herself. In mid-rant, she hears a tap on her window. She turns and looks up into the barrel of a gun held by a very serious police officer. He orders her to turn off the engine, keep her hands in sight, and exit the vehicle. The speechless woman does exactly what the policeman orders. Getting out of the car, she places her hands on the roof. The policeman replaces his gun in its holster and locks her wrists in handcuffs. She is hustled into the officer's patrol car and taken to the station where she is fingerprinted, photographed, searched, booked and placed in a holding cell to wait. She is too bewildered and frightened to ask any questions.

A couple of hours later, the desk sergeant comes to the cell and opens the door. She is escorted back to the booking area where the arresting officer is waiting with her personal effects.

"I'm very sorry for the mistake, ma'am," he explains as he returns her handbag. "But you see, I pulled up behind your car while you were blowing your horn, swearing, and making obscene gestures at the guy in front of you. Then I noticed the *We worship at St. Joseph's* license plate holder, the *What Would Jesus Do?* bumper sticker and the chrome-plated Christian fish emblem on the trunk. So, naturally … I assumed you had stolen the car."

The connection between the values we profess on our bumpers and the values we "drive" is the focus of today's Gospel, the conclusion of Jesus' "Sermon on the Plain" in Luke's Gospel. Jesus invokes here a style of preaching known as *charaz* — "stringing beads." Luke has "strung" three of Jesus' "beads" together as his final exhortation to the crowds who have gathered on the plain:

"The blind leading the blind": Jesus admonishes his disciples not to judge or condemn but to seek reconciliation and community with others. God's mercy and compassion is the light in which we find our own way to God; by reflecting that light in our own lives others can then find their way to God, as well.

"No disciple is superior to the teacher": Becoming a disciple is a constant process of discernment and conversion. The disciple never "surpasses" his/her instruction; nor is the disciple ever "better" than those he/she brings to God. Our embrace of the Gospel does not make us any better in the eyes of God or the world; baptism does not induct us into some kind of exclusive club or make us one of the ruling elite. We are always students of Christ, the Teacher of humility and reconciliation. In imitating Christ's forgiveness and compassion, we do not become the superiors of others; we only live up to our call to be their brothers and sisters under the providence of God.

"Remove the wooden beam from your eye first": Authentic discipleship begins with confronting within ourselves both the good and the evil we are capable of and the values that compel us to think, speak and act as we do. Like trying to remove "the splinter" in another's eye, targeting scapegoats does not solve problems; judging motives remedies nothing; condemnations are useless. Jesus calls his disciples to seek personal conversion and reconciliation with others first — removing the "wooden beams" from our own eyes first. The "splinters" in others will follow.

Today's pericope concludes with the parable of the fruitful tree: We cannot speak sincerely or effectively of God with our lips unless God is present in our heart. We will not be judged by the "fruit" we "planned" to harvest nor by the fruit we "could have" yielded if it weren't for a lack of time, a tough boss, an unfair teacher, a childhood of poverty, etc.; we will be known before God by the "yield" we work for and dedicate ourselves to harvesting for the love of God.

Christ our light,
help us to see beyond the splinters and wood beams
to see you in one another.
Plant and nurture the seed of your compassion
in our hearts
so that we may realize one day
the harvest of your justice and mercy.

Sunday 9 / Proper 3

A centurion in Capernaum had a slave who was ill and about to die, and he was valuable to him. "Lord, do not trouble yourself, for I am not worthy to have you enter under my roof ... but say the word and let my servant be healed."

Luke 7: 1–10

From a child's vantage point

On a busy Saturday morning, Dad and his five-year-old son Martin made a bargain: If Martin behaved himself while Dad ran some errands at the home improvement store, Dad would take Martin to a movie. Deal!

But the deal quickly fell apart. Martin began to pout and whine as soon as he and Dad walked into the store, making it impossible for Dad to get anything done.

"I don't think you're holding up your end of the bargain, buddy," Dad said. "We had a deal. Remember?"

The little boy nodded tearfully.

Dad noticed that Martin's shoelaces had come undone and knelt down to tie them. Martin sniffled as he grabbed the sleeve of his father's sweatshirt, holding on. From his knees, Dad now could see the chaos around them: Shoppers nudged and pushed one another in an effort to get through the aisles; an hysterical mother called out for a lost child; a display of boxed items tumbled to the floor because a distracted customer wheeled a cart into it. And poor Martin kept getting bumped in the shoulders and head with purses and bags as people brushed passed him.

At his little boy's eye level, Dad saw how overwhelming and terrifying all of this chaos was to a five-year-old. He felt awful for not having been more sympathetic to his son's plight and realized that Martin had been a champ in trying to brave his way through it all.

Shoes tied, Dad lifted up Martin and placed him on his shoulders. "What do you say we get out of here and do this shopping some other time?"

"Are you sure, Daddy?" Martin asked, trying to gauge why the plan was changing.

"Yup. Positive. Let's go to that movie."

Compassion is the ability to put oneself in the place of another: to see the world from their perspective, to see what scares them, to understand their fears, to embrace their pain. For Luke, the centurion in today's Gospel models such compassion.

The equivalent of a sergeant (centurions were considered the "backbone" of the Roman Army), the centurion, as a foreigner, would be typically denounced as "unclean" by observant Jews; but because of the respect he has shown for the beliefs and values of their faith, this centurion is held in high regard by the Jews. Despite the deeply-etched class distinctions of his highly secular Roman culture, the centurion is clearly a man of great compassion, whose kindness and care are extended even to one of his slaves — someone who was considered, under the law, as property, not entitled to even the most basic human rights. Jesus is moved at the centurion's righteousness, which contrasts sharply with the disbelief of the people of the covenant he has encountered. Jesus exalts the "unclean" officer's humility and trust by curing his slave.

The centurion is a model of greatness as Jesus defines greatness: a leader who sees his authority as a responsibility to serve others and enable others to realize their own lives' potential to serve. Too often we see people as merely numbers and statistics, as markets and demographics; we value others because of the role they play, their productivity and service, their usefulness to us in our plans and successes; we define them quickly and mercilessly by their class or race or ethnicity or religion. The story of the centurion in Luke's Gospel challenges us to look beyond labels and stereotypes to see fellow human beings — all sons and daughters of God, our brothers and sisters in Christ. Jesus calls us to recognize and reach out to those whom the world dismisses as unimportant, needless and marginal and welcome them into our midst as God's own.

Compassionate God,
open our eyes to see you in the faces of the poor,
  the troubled and the forgotten;
open our hands to reach out to them
  in your hope and peace.
May we give you thanks for all your blessings to us
by seeking to share those blessings
  with all our brothers and sisters in Christ Jesus.

When the Lord saw the widow, he was moved with pity for her and said to her, "Do not weep." He stepped forward and touched the coffin; at this the bearers halted, and he said, "Young man, I tell you, arise!"

Luke 7: 11–17

"The Jesus factor"

A science professor had a no-nonsense method for assigning grades in his courses. A student's final letter grade was based on how many points the student had accumulated during the semester. The points, in turn, could be earned in a variety of ways: daily quizzes, lab reports, a lengthy midterm, and a final exam. If, by the time of the final, a student had already built up enough points for a B or C, and if the student was content with that grade, he or she could skip the final. Or the student could take it easy early on, skipping quizzes and lab reports, and hope that by cramming the student could get the points needed on one of the big tests.

The instructor, who also let it be known that he had no use for religious beliefs, had a clever way of introducing his points-system to his classes. "There is no Jesus factor in this course," he would announce.

A former student of this teacher, now a college professor himself, remembers:

"I have often wished that I had asked him what he meant exactly by a 'Jesus factor.' But I think I have some idea. He wanted to eliminate all subjective factors in his grading. In his classroom, you got what your earned, and what it took was clearly spelled out … *No excuses: Show me the points!* In a word, there is no room for mercy in his system, and he was proud of it.

"Actually, his system worked quite well. He may have been too rigid in his attitudes, but his total-points method was quite appropriate for a biology course. But I'm glad when it comes to dealing with the larger issues of life, there is indeed a Jesus factor. Mercy is what the Gospel is really all about. If the Lord were simply to add up the points earned, we would all be miserable failures.… I am glad that when we all face the real final test — the Last Judgment — God isn't going to pass me or fail me on my ability to show the points. On that Day, the Jesus factor will be my only hope."[3]

"The Jesus factor" is constantly at work throughout Luke's Gospel. The raising up of the widow's son in the village of Nain is a case in point. This story underlines two key themes of Luke's Gospel: the extraordinary love and compassion of Jesus for the poor and destitute (widows are the epitome of need and despair in Scripture) and Jesus as the great fulfillment of Israel's Messianic hope when "the eyes of the blind will be opened, the ears of the deaf unstopped, the lame shall leap like a deer, and the tongue of the speechless sing for joy" (Isaiah 35: 5–6). Luke refers to Jesus here as "Lord," the Old Testament Greek title for the Holy One who is Master of life and death.

The word compassion literally means "to suffer with." Compassion is the "Jesus factor" that inspires true discipleship: the Jesus of compassion challenges us to bring hope and healing to others, without condition or considering the cost, only because they are brothers and sisters of us in the same Father.

Instill in us, O Lord,
your wisdom and grace,
that your Gospel of compassion may be
the measure of all our decision-making,
the lens through which we see one another,
the destination we journey toward every day.

A woman stood behind Jesus at his feet weeping and began to bathe his feet with her tears. Then she wiped them with her hair, kissed them, and anointed them with the ointment … Jesus said to Simon, "Her many sins have been forgiven because she has shown great love."

Luke 7: 36 – 8: 3

Dodie

In his book *On Writing: A Memoir of the Craft,* Stephen King recounts the sad story of Dodie Franklin, a girl he went to school with in Lisbon Falls, Maine. Dodie's tragic life inspired his horror classic *Carrie.*

Dodie was one of the loneliest, most reviled girls in the class. The other girls called her "Dodo" or "Doodoo." Dodie was painfully shy; her parents seemed to have no time or interest in her or her brother. Everyday she wore the same outfit to school: a long black skirt, gray-knee socks and a white blouse. The other girls made fun of her — at first behind her back and then to her face. Teasing became taunting. They didn't just laugh at Dodie — they hated her, too. Dodie was everything they were afraid of.

After Christmas vacation during her sophomore year, Dodie came back to school looking resplendent. The long, dowdy black skirt was replaced by a cranberry-colored one that stopped stylishly at her knees. The tatty knee socks were replaced with nylons. The ancient white blouse gave way to a soft wool sweater. She even had a permanent. Dodie was a girl transformed, and you could see by her face that she knew it.

But the new clothes and hairstyle changed nothing.

"The teasing that day was worse than ever," King writes. "Her peers had no intention of letting her out of the box they'd put her in; she was punished for even trying to break free. I had several classes with her and was able to observe Dodie's ruination first hand. I saw her smile fade, saw the light in her eyes first dim and then go out. By the end of the day she was the girl she'd been before Christmas vacation — a dough-faced and freckle-cheeked wraith, scurrying through the halls with her eyes down and her books clasped to her chest."

She wore her "new" clothes every day, until they became as faded and worn, as matted and dispirited, as her "old" clothes. The home permanent wasn't repeated. Her brief happiness was forever destroyed, her momentary radiance effectively snuffed out for good.

"[Dodie] had made a break for the fence and had to be knocked down, that was all. Once the escape was foiled and the entire company of prisoners was once more accounted for, life could go back to normal."

In today's Gospel, while Simon and his guests are appalled at her boldness, Jesus graciously accepts the penitent woman's act of loving hospitality. In doing so, Jesus transforms her humiliation into joy, her ridiculous display into a prayerful offering. Again and again in Luke's Gospel we see Jesus lifting people out of the boxes in which they have been placed: from the most despised tax collector to the poorest serving girl, Jesus calls forth and lifts up the goodness each one of them possesses — even the condemned criminal hanging next to him on Calvary will be promised paradise for the compassion he extends to the dying Jesus.

The woman's attitude stands in stark contrast to the calculated reserve of the proper Simon, who believes that Jesus has disgraced himself by acknowledging this pitiful display; but Simon fails to understand everyone's need — including his own — for forgiveness and reconciliation with those we hurt and who hurt us. We all need "five hundred days' wages" worth of forgiveness, but we may be too blind to our sinfulness or too afraid or too proud to ask that our debt be written off. Only in acknowledging that need are we able to experience the loving forgiveness of God the penitent woman receives at the feet of Jesus.

"Polite" society of Luke's time had little regard for women (through the centuries, readers of Luke have assumed the woman in the story was guilty of some sexual sin, but there is nothing in the text to suggest that). Throughout his Gospel, Luke exalts the role and gifts of women. In the final verses of today's Gospel (Luke 8: 2–3), Luke identifies two of the women who will be among the first witnesses of Jesus' resurrection: Mary, called Magdalene, was a poor, mentally ill woman cured by Jesus; Joanna, the wife of Herod's chief steward and manager, was a woman of considerable position and means. Both women, though of very different backgrounds, find sisterhood and community in the presence of the compassionate Jesus.

Every one of us — whether Pharisee to serving girl — is in need of forgiveness, of healing the hurts that estrange us from others. As disciples of Jesus, we are called to be reconcilers, not judges; we are called to forgive, not to keep score; we are called to welcome back those who want to return and to enable them to put their lives back together, not to set up conditions or establish litmus tests to prove their sincerity. Sadly, no one offered such transformation to poor Dodie (who, King remembers, died young and alone after the birth of her second child). As Jesus transforms the lives of those marginalized, forgotten and used by society, so we are called to do the same: to welcome and honor the poor and struggling, the lost and broken in our midst, and to realize, in all humility, how we are all in need of the forgiveness and acceptance we can find at the feet of Jesus.

God of compassion,
in his selfless and humble emptying of himself for us,
your Son transformed our lives from despair to hope,
from pain to wholeness, from sadness to joy,
from death to life.
May we never fear to imitate
his healing of the victimized and ridiculed,
his lifting up of the fallen and afraid,
his seeking out those driven away and lost.

When he saw Jesus, the possessed man cried out and fell down before him; in a loud voice, he shouted, "What have you to do with me, Jesus, Son of the Most High God? I beg you, do not torment me!" A herd of many swine was feeding there on the hillside, and the demons pleaded with Jesus to allow them to enter the swine; and he let them.

Luke 8: 26–39

The Great Divorce

In his book *The Great Divorce,* C.S. Lewis takes readers on an imaginary trip through heaven and hell.

In the course of the journey, a soul comes to heaven with a little red lizard on his shoulder. The snarling reptile twitches its tail like a whip and whispers all kinds of horrible things in the poor soul's ear.

An angel appears and invites the soul into heaven for eternity, but the soul demurs. "Thank you for your hospitality," the soul says, "but it's no good, you see. I told this little chap that he'd have to be quiet if he came — which he insisted on doing. Of course his stuff won't do here: I realize that. But he won't stop. I'll just have to go home."

"Would you like me to make him quiet?" the angel offers.

"Of course I would!"

"Then I will kill him," the angel says.

But the soul is horrified. "You didn't say anything about killing him. I hardly meant to bother you with anything so drastic."

"But it's the only way," the angel says, moving closer to the vile little creature. "Shall I kill it?"

The soul steps back. "Well, I'm quite open to considering it. I mean, I was only thinking about silencing it because up here — well, it's so embarrassing.... Please, I never meant to be such a nuisance. Please — really — don't bother. Look! It's gone to sleep of its own accord. I'm sure it'll be all right. Thanks ever so much."

But the angel explains that the lizard is keeping the soul from the kingdom of heaven. As the angel steps closer to the lizard, the lizard screams to the soul, "Be careful! He can do what he says. He can kill me. One fatal word from you and he will! Then you'll be without me for ever and ever.... I'll give you nothing but really nice dreams — all sweet and fresh and almost innocent.... "

The angel pleads with the soul to let him destroy the lizard.

The soul is caught between the heaven he so wants to enter and the lizard he is afraid to give up. The tortured soul finally surrenders. "Do what you will!" the soul wails, convinced that he will be destroyed as well the lizard.

The angel pulls the lizard off the soul's shoulder, twists its body and throws it to the ground. Suddenly, the broken lizard is transformed into a magnificent stallion — and the terrified soul has been re-created into the same beautiful form as the angel. The re-created man then happily climbs on the back of the stallion and together they ride into heaven.

The lizard, C.S. Lewis' guide explains, is the poor soul's self-centeredness that prevents him from embracing the love of God. Only by killing the lizard of all that is sinful within him can the soul rise to the life of God.

C.S. Lewis' tale mirrors the eerie scene in today's Gospel. A madman — naked, given to violent seizures, left to stalking cemeteries, deprived of family, friends and identity — shouts at Jesus as he is going by. When Jesus meets the man, the demons themselves speak. Once Jesus subjugates them, they beg to enter into a nearby herd of pigs, which then rush down the hillside into the lake where they drown.

This story reflects a common theme of Luke's Gospel: Jesus' compassion trumps empty rituals and blindly-followed social convention. The psychotic man, considered "unclean" and ritually impure by religious Jews, is condemned to live among the tombs. In Luke's account (unlike Matthew and Mark's version of the story), Jesus commands the spirits to leave him before the man can ask Jesus for healing. In demanding to know the name of the demons, Jesus demonstrates his authority over them. In ancient thought, to know a name was to exercise control, and so the demons freely surrender to Jesus' authority, realizing that they must be obedient to him.

The name Legion is the technical term for a division of five thousand Roman soldiers, suggesting the large horde of demons possessing the man. For Jesus' Jewish hearers, pigs epitomized both paganism and their hated Roman occupiers. Rather than return to the "abyss" (the realm of Satan), the demons ask that they be allowed to enter the pigs on the nearby hillside; Jesus agrees, but then plummets the herd into the lake, marking visible proof that the demons have left the man once and for all.

Jesus' authority displayed here is not an "authority" constructed of legend and celebrity. His authority over good and evil is centered in the selfless, limitless and unconditional love of God and the spirit of humility that seeks to put the power of one's "authority" at the service of others. The man, now healed, is sent by Jesus to proclaim the goodness of God throughout the town, becoming one of the first Gentile missionaries. But those who witness this exorcism are terrified at the power of this Jesus and ask him to leave.

We all have "lizards" distracting us from the things of God; we are all "possessed" by "demons" that kill our hopes and mire us in deadening cynicism. Yet we hesitate to be rid of them: our lizards and demons protect the comfortable and secure little "tombs" we have constructed for ourselves isolating us from whatever terrifies us or challenges us. But Christ comes to exorcise those demons and transform those lizards that we may be made new and whole in the limitless compassion of God.

Healing Christ,
cast out of our own hearts and spirits
those "demons" that separate us from God
and the things of God:

the demons of fear, of ignorance, of greed, of selfishness,
of hatred.
Kill the "lizards" that control us and manipulate us,
that enable us to rationalize our acting in ways
contrary to the Gospel we profess,
transforming them into spirits of selfless compassion
and merciful forgiveness.

Sunday 13 / Proper 8

"No one who sets a hand to the plow and looks to what was left behind is fit for the kingdom of God."

Luke 9: 51–62

The kind of player you can't coach

A tall, gangly, self-conscious seventh-grader was on her junior high girls' track team. A meet scheduled for one Saturday had to be postponed to the following Saturday — when the girl's church had planned a community service project that she had signed up for. She went to her track coach and told him about the conflict. He told her, "Your teammates are counting on you and you can't let them down. I expect you to be here for the meet."

She went home in tears. The next day she talked to him again; he responded, "You are either here for the meet or you turn in your uniform."

After a sleepless, tearful night, she made her decision.

The next day she went to the coach's office, handed him her uniform and walked away.

Her parents and the parents of her teammates were surprised and even shocked: their own teenage daughter was actually choosing God and church over her track team, even though that was the way they raised her.

The girl said simply, "This is about God."[4]

This teenager makes a hard decision regarding her own sense of discipleship. Today's Gospel focuses on the difficult demands of being an authentic follower of Jesus.

Jesus proceeds to Jerusalem to take up the cross that awaits him there (Jerusalem is the focus of the second half of Luke's Gospel). He travels through Samaria — the most direct route to the Holy City but usually avoided by Jews. The hatred between the Jews and the Samaritans dated back to the eighth century BC, when

Assyria conquered northern Israel (Samaria). Those northerners who survived the disaster intermarried with foreigners resettled by the Assyrians. The Jews of Jerusalem considered such accommodation treason and, worse, a betrayal of the holy faith; they considered the Samaritan population too mixed to be considered still part of the covenant. Jerusalem banned the Samaritans from the temple and synagogues, refused their religious contributions and denied their legal status in court proceedings. The spurned Samaritans maintained their own form of Judaic religious practice (holding only to the books of Genesis, Exodus, Leviticus, Numbers and Deuteronomy) centered on Mount Gerizim in Shechem.

Most Jews avoided the territories of the Samaritans, who would do everything they could to hinder and even attack pilgrims to Jerusalem. Jesus, however, proceeds through Samaria, regardless of their inhospitality and responds to their bitterness with tolerance and reconciliation.

Along the way, three would-be disciples ask to join Jesus. To the first, Jesus asks if he clearly understands the cost of discipleship; Jesus urges the second not to find excuses or rationalizations for avoiding the call of God; Jesus reminds the third that discipleship demands a total dedication and commitment to seeking God in all things.

The seventh-grader responds to the responsibility of discipleship with the clear, unhesitating, unambiguous and total commitment that Jesus asks of anyone who would be his disciple. There can be no "but first … ," no "in a minute," no "on second thought." Jesus' Gospel is not a collection of pious aphorisms but a God-centered perspective for seeing ourselves and our world and an attitude by which we live our lives. We cannot be disciples by being mere spectators of God's presence; possessing a baptismal certificate alone does not mark us as disciples of the Risen One. Jesus calls those who would be his disciples not to look back with regret or fear to what we leave undone but to look forward to the possibilities we have to establish and build the reign of God in our own time and place.

As the seventh-grader runner realizes, following Jesus means taking on the hard work and courage of making the reign of God a reality — regardless of the cost, regardless of the difficulty, regardless of the sacrifice.

Lord Jesus,
may we walk with you on the road to Jerusalem.
In following your humble way of compassion,
   forgiveness and justice,
may we be worthy of being called your disciple.
With your hand on ours,
with the strength of your grace,
may we put our hands to the plow,
looking forward with hope
   to the planting of your reign
in our own time and place.

"Into whatever house you enter, first say, 'Peace to this household.' "

Luke 10: 1–12, 17–20

The search for the magic seed

There is an old Chinese tale about a woman whose only son died. In her grief, she pleaded with a monk renowned for his holiness: "What prayers, what magical incantations do you have to bring my son back to life?"

Instead of sending her away or trying to reason with her, the monk said, "Fetch me a mustard seed from a home that has never known sorrow. We will use it to drive the sorrow out of your life."

The woman set off at once in search of the magical mustard seed. She came first to a splendid mansion, knocked at the door, and said, "I am looking for a home that has never known sorrow. Is this such a place? It is very important to me."

They told her, "You've certainly come to the wrong place," and then began to describe to her the tragic things that had befallen their household.

The woman said to herself, "Who is better able to help these poor unfortunate people than I who have had misfortune of my own?" She stayed to offer what help and comfort she could, then went on in her search for a home that had never known sorrow.

But wherever she stopped, whether hovels and palaces, she found one tale after another of sadness and misfortune. Ultimately, she became so involved in ministering to other people's grief that she forgot her quest for the magical mustard seed, never realizing that, in her compassion, she possessed the "magic" seed all along.

Today's Gospel is about our own journeys for the "magic seed." Jesus commissions 72 messengers (some ancient manuscripts record 70) to go before him to prepare for his arrival in the towns along his route to Jerusalem. In keeping with Luke's use of symbolic numbers and his Gentile perspective, the 72 disciples represent the new Church's mission to every nation and people under heaven (the number 72 symbolized for the Jews the number of the world's Gentile nations).

Jesus instructs the seventy-two:

- to keep focused on the ways and values of God — travel light, accept the simple hospitality of those they visit, and offer blessings and gratitude to their hosts (in keeping with the traditions of Middle Eastern hospitality);
- to proclaim God's peace "amid wolves";
- to offer hope and healing, not judgment and condemnation;
- to find satisfaction not in what they have done in God's name but to rejoice in what God has done through them.

Today's reading concludes with the seventy-two returning from their mission rejoicing in their apparent success in conquering the "demons" they have encountered on their travels. Empowered by Jesus, they have become co-workers in building the kingdom of the Father.

Jesus commissions the seventy-two disciples of the Gospel — and us — to proclaim peace: peace that is centered in embracing Christ's attitude of servanthood and his spirit of compassion, peace that enables us to bring forth the good that exists within everyone, peace that is returned to us in extending the blessing of that peace to others. As the grieving woman discovers in her search for the magic seed, it is in extending such blessings to others that we behold the sign of God's love and become that sign for others.

Lord God,
you are both the road we follow
  and the destination of our journey.
With grace as our travel bag
and peace as our walking stick,
may we discover your love and healing along the way.
By the compassion and peace we are able to offer,
may we cast out demons of fear,
  estrangement and injustice;
may we become seeds of your peace and grace
in our homes and schools and workplaces.

Sunday 15 / Proper 10

The parable of the Good Samaritan: " … a Samaritan traveler who came upon him was moved with compassion at the sight."

Luke 10: 25–37

Warming the coldest heart

A cold wave swept through a small Russian village, making life miserable for the poor and homeless. On a bitterly cold day, the rabbi went to the home of the town's wealthiest man, seeking help for his desperate congregants.

The rabbi knocked and the rich man opened the door. "Come in, Rabbi," the rich man invited. Unlike everyone else in town, the man was in shirtsleeves; after all, his house was well heated.

"No," the rabbi said. "No need for me to come in. I'll just be a minute." And the rabbi proceeded to engage the rich man in a lengthy, rambling conversation. The rabbi asked him about his family and how all were faring during this difficult time. Standing at his doorstep, the rich man was freezing, but every time he asked the rabbi to come inside, the rabbi demurred.

The rabbi went on and on.

"And how is your wife's cousin, the lumber merchant? And your sister and her family — are they coping well in this bitter weather?"

By this time the rich man's cheeks were red with cold. "Rabbi, what did you come here for?" he finally demanded.

"Oh, that," the rabbi said. "I've come to ask for your help to buy coal for the poor people in town."

"So why don't you come in and we'll talk about it?"

"Because if I come in, we will sit down by your fireplace. You will be very warm and comfortable, and when I tell you how the poor are suffering from the cold, you really won't understand. You will give me a few rubles and send me on my way. But now, out here," the rabbi went on, pointing to the frozen moisture in the rich man's eyes and along his cheeks, "when I tell you how the poor are suffering from the cold, I think you will understand better."

The man was happy to give the rabbi a hundred rubles just so he could shut the door and return to his fireplace.

A lawyer's question about who is — and, by implication, who is *not* — one's neighbor sets the stage for one of Jesus' most beloved parables, the story of the Good Samaritan (found only in Luke's Gospel). Jesus stuns his hearers by making a Samaritan the hero of the story — especially in light of the inhospitality of the Samaritans during their journey to Jerusalem (see notes for Sunday 13/Proper 8). Jesus' hearers would expect a Samaritan to be the villain of the story, not the hero. While the two clerics do not help the man for fear of violating the Torah by being defiled by the dead, the compassionate Samaritan — a man presumably with little concern for Jewish belief or morality, an unwelcome outsider in this region — is so moved by the plight of the poor man that he thinks nothing of stopping to help regardless of the cost of time or money.

The Jews of Jesus' time defined "neighbor" exclusively as other Jews, but Jesus' parable expands such a limited perspective. The Samaritan and the traveler illustrate that Jesus' concept of "neighbor" is not limited to one's own clan or community. Christ-like compassion must be manifested in deeds of kindness; morality, in the light of the Gospel, cannot be guided by laws inscribed in stone but ultimately by the spirit of the heart.

The parable of the Good Samaritan calls us to embrace a vision of faith that sees every man, woman and child — regardless of whatever labels society has assigned to them — as our "neighbors." Christ calls us who would be his disciples to step outside our warm houses to experience for ourselves the cold endured by the poor and homeless; to give from our own poverty to alleviate the hunger of those whose larders are empty; to place on our own mounts the victims of economic and emotional circumstances beyond their control; to see our own wealth as a means to bring healing and hope into the lives who have little. The Good Samaritan is the model of Gospel charity, the embodiment of the Gospel vision of humanity as a community of everyone — male and female, rich and poor, able and challenged — sharing the same sacred dignity as sons and daughters of the God of all that is good.

Open our eyes, O God,
to recognize you in one another;
open our hands
to reach out to others in peace and generosity;
open our hearts
to welcome to our tables and hearths
all men and woman as our brothers and sisters,
your sons and daughters.

Sunday 16 / Proper 11

"Martha, Martha, you are anxious and worried about many things. There is need of only one thing. Mary has chosen the better part and it will not be taken from her."

Luke 10: 38–42

Two sisters

Luke's Gospel recounts the tiff between two very different sisters: Martha, the practical, no-nonsense housekeeper, and Mary, the romantic "free spirit" who is captivated by the charismatic Jesus. For Martha, there is a household to run, beds to be made, meals to be cooked and served; for Mary, nothing else matters because Jesus is in their midst. It is easy to understand the tension that could arise between two very different women.

But, in our own experience, Martha and Mary can be and often are found within the same person. There is something of both Martha and Mary within each one of us — and the conflict between the two is just as real.

Our "Martha" side is consumed with the work and necessities of living and surviving in the modern world: careers to establish, mortgages to repay, food and clothing to pay for, college tuitions to cover; but the "Mary" within us longs to spend more time with our children, to be able to give more of ourselves to causes we believe in, to turn off the world and be at peace with God, ourselves and everyone else. The "Martha" is always there to remind us of our responsibilities: the "things to do" list that is never completed, the calendar that is always full, the deadlines that always loom — there simply aren't enough hours in the day to possess the "the better part." But our "Mary" side seeks something more meaningful and purposeful in our lives.

The sisters Martha and Mary mirror the two expressions of the disciple's call: loving service to others (Martha) and prayer and contemplation (Mary). But as Martha comes to realize in today's Gospel, discipleship begins with hearing the Word of God, with opening our hearts and spirits to the presence of God. "The better part" embraced by Mary transcends the pragmatic and practical concerns of the everyday (that have overwhelmed poor Martha) and sees the hand of God in all things and realizes the gratitude all of creation owes its loving Creator for the gift of life.

"The better part" is not what is left over when everything else is done — it is not the "cheese" at the end of the maze we race through. We have to consciously choose and seek out "the better part." Like Martha, we can become so obsessed with and distracted by the business and "busy-ness" of life that we become anesthetized to feeling and experiencing "the better part."

Jesus invites each one of us to make a place in our lives for the "better part" — the joy and love of family and friends that is the manifestation of God's presence in our lives.

In the midst of the many demands made on us,
Lord Jesus,
help us to recognize "the better part":
may we seek to love rather than to be loved,
may we live lives of integrity rather than accommodation,
may we find joy in giving rather than taking,
may we find fulfillment in being a part of
rather than being in control.
In the noise around us, may we hear your voice;
in the challenges we face, may we seek your light;
in the chasms that divide us, may we seek your healing.

"When you pray, say, Father, hallowed be your name, your kingdom come ... If you who are wicked know how to give good gifts to your children, how much more will the Father in heaven give the Holy Spirit to those who ask him?"

Luke 11: 1–13

Prayer in the midst of the garbage

A man discovered that he had lost his wedding ring. He was beside himself — after all, that band wasn't just a piece of jewelry but a symbol of the life he shared with his beloved wife, of their love and devotion to one another, victorious in bad times and glorious in good times.

He searched everywhere, crawling around the woodpile, emptying vacuum bags, taking the seats out of the car, probing the tight spaces between sofa cushions. Nothing. Every step of the search included the prayer: *Please, God, this is important to me.*

Then, as he was washing his hands in the kitchen sink, the family cat jumped up on the counter, knocking a spoon into the wastebasket below. He suddenly remembered: He had taken off his ring to do the dishes, placing it in the same spot where the cat had just landed. The cat had knocked the ring into the wastebasket.

When he told his wife, her face turned pale. "You've already taken our garbage to the town dumpster."

The man raced to the town dumpster, but it had already been emptied. He then went to the rubbish removal company and explained his plight to the clerk. "But, sir, tons of refuse have been already compacted and put on the truck to be taken to the landfill tomorrow."

The man persisted. Could he go to the dump and look?

The clerk got on the phone to the landfill office. "Could our driver unload tomorrow in an area that is relatively flat and clean?

We've got a guy here who wants to find something he's lost." The landfill people couldn't believe it either, but they agreed.

The next day, a gray, sleeting November afternoon, the man drove behind the truck to the landfill site. The driver unloaded the garbage: it was a wall of refuse six feet high and maybe 70 feet long. The man was devastated. But the driver jumped down from the cab, and said, "Okay, where do we start?"

"We?" the man asked. "You're going to help me dig through this?"

"Sure. I think your dumpster load should be somewhere around here."

They started wading through a sea of garbage, the freezing rain pouring down their necks. "We're never going to find that ring!" the man shouted. "Don't say never," the driver yelled back. "You're going to find it."

The man and the driver plowed through the mountain of garbage, all the time praying his prayer: *Please, God, this is important to me.*

The man then spotted a blue-gray circle — the color of paint the man had just used to paint the shutters of his house. It was the paint can. The two rummaged through several bags. The man yanked open one bag and found a crushed egg carton — and nestled in an indentation was the ring. The man and the driver howled with joy.

That evening, the man and his wife celebrated by going out to dinner. At the table, she slipped the ring back on his finger. "With this ring," she said softly, "I thee wed."

"You know, honey, everybody thought I was nuts for going to all that trouble."

"I didn't," she smiled.[5]

The Shaker tradition has a saying that puts the concept of prayer this simply: "Hearts to God, hands to work." *Hearts to God* — seeking God's vision; *hands to work* — making that vision a reality.

In today's reading from Luke's Gospel, the disciples ask Jesus to teach them how to pray. What is important to grasp are not the words of the prayer (Luke's version of the Lord's Prayer is shorter and more concise than Matthew's version), but the attitude of prayer Jesus teaches. To pray is not to impose our will on God but to ask God to make us open to his will; in other words, we pray not to change God's mind but for God to change ours.

Authentic prayer, as taught by Jesus and contained in The Lord's Prayer, has three elements:

Acknowledging the goodness and love of God: Jesus teaches us to call God "Father." God is not the cosmic tyrant out of whom gifts have to be extracted through humiliating pleading; he is the loving eternal Parent who delights in providing for his children's needs.

Asking that we may do God's will: Prayer worthy of God asks for the grace to do his work of forgiveness, reconciliation and, to become the brothers and sisters he calls us to become under his providence.

Voicing our hope in the providence of God: We come before God knowing that, just as parents will provide for their children and a friend will come to the aid of a friend, God will hear our prayers and give us what we need and more. Even if it seems as if our prayers are unanswered, we live with the confident faith that God is always present to us.

Hearts to God, hands to work. The man searching for his wedding ring prays — and his prayer is answered not with a miraculous GPS signal to his ring but with the grace to scale a mountain of garbage to find it. Christ teaches us that real prayer does not ask God for miracles but asks God for the courage and perseverance to make our own.

Father, hear our prayers —
prayers that you know before we ask them,
prayers you inspire us to ask.
Let our prayers to you transform us:
making us more grateful,
more forgiving,
more caring of one another.
In your goodness, give us the grace and trust
to work to make what we ask of you a reality.

The parable of the foolish rich man: "You fool, this night your life will be demanded of you; and the things you have prepared, to whom will they belong?"

Luke 12: 13–21

Home ownership

Two families asked their village's rabbi to settle a dispute about the boundaries of their land.

The rabbi listened to the members of one family recount how they inherited the land from their ancestors and how it had been in the family for many generations; they produced documents and maps to prove their claim.

Then the rabbi listened to the other family describe how they had lived on the land for many years, working it and harvesting it. They claimed that they knew the land intimately; they had no papers to prove their claim, only their calloused hands and sore backs and the harvest they reaped from the land.

After presenting their cases, the families said, "Decide, Rabbi, who owns this land."

The rabbi said nothing. He knelt down on the land and put his ear to the ground. He listened for some time. He then stood up and said to the two families, "I have listened to both of you, but I had to listen to the land, the center of the dispute, and the land has spoken. It has told me this: 'Neither of you owns the land you stand on. It is the land that owns you.'"

In Gospel times, rabbis were often asked to arbitrate conflicts within families and communities. In today's Gospel, the rabbi Jesus has been approached to settle an argument over an inheritance, but he refuses to be cast in the role of arbiter. Jesus responds not by taking sides but by addressing the greed that has brought both sides to near blows. He tells the parable of the rich man who, in the midst of his good fortune, loses his sense of what is important.

Possessions create the illusion that we can control our lives; the drive for gain makes us oblivious to the needs and dreams of others. The "foolish" rich man in today's Gospel sadly discovers that wealth in the reign of God has nothing to do with stock portfolios, bank accounts or the social register.

We are often as shortsighted as the rich farmer in today's Gospel: we can become so self-centered and self-sufficient that we shut ourselves off from the seemingly simple aspects of life in which we find the love and presence of God. We can be "owned" by the things we think we own: We become so obsessed with obtaining the most elegant home, the newest car, the most stylish clothes, the latest technological gadgets that our possessions *own* us, confiscating all of our time and energy to buy and maintain them. The most devastating poverty is the emptiness of a life filled with things but possessing nothing of God nor the things of God: love, forgiveness, compassion, gratitude.

Our lives are not about amassing fortunes or achieving great celebrity; our lives are about finding and embracing selfless and affirming love, about discovering how to love one another as God loves us: totally and completely, without condition nor limit.

God of every good thing,
instill in us a spirit of poverty —
not an austere hatred for the things of the world
but an appreciation for the many gifts
you have given us
and a commitment to use what you have given us
to establish your reign of compassion and forgiveness,
of justice and peace.
Fill our homes with joy and love;
fill our barns with an unending capacity
for generosity and kindness
to all who come to our table.

Sunday 19 / Proper 14

The parable of the foolish servant awaiting his master's return: "For where your treasure is, there also will your heart be ... You also must be prepared, for at an hour you do not expect, the Son of Man will come ... Much will be required of the person entrusted with much, and still more will be demanded of the person entrusted with more."

Luke 12: 32–48
[Roman lectionary]

Luke 12: 32–40
[Common lectionary]

Finding your treasure

Take a few minutes and read over the pages of your calendar book or scroll through your Blackberry. It may surprise you to see how you spend God's most precious gift to you: time. It's humbling and a little disconcerting to discover the time you devote to appointments and projects — all so terribly important at the moment — at the expense of time spent with family and friends, time spent doing the kind of charity work that stretches your soul, time spent with God. *For how you spend your time, there also will your heart be....*

Most of us dread that April showdown with the I.R.S. — but it can be a revelation. Reviewing the past year's income and bank statements, expenses, receipts and donations is a pretty good indicator of where your money goes — and what's most important to you. *For where you spend your money, there also will your heart be....*

Stop and take a look at the data you keep at your fingertips: the contacts in your Rolodex, the family's schedules posted on the refrigerator, the websites you have bookmarked. *For where your energy is spent and your attention is focused, there also will your heart be....*

Frederick Douglass said that "a man is worked *upon* by what he works *on.* He may carve out his circumstances, but his circumstances will carve him out as well." Today's Gospel echoes that same theme: The work we do and the lives we create, in turn, form the values we embrace and the moral and ethic core we live. How we spend our time, how we use our wealth, how we focus our energy are the true indicators of what we treasure. Too often what we say we value is betrayed by the busyness of our days; the demands on our time and resources undermine the values we believe in the depth of our hearts

In three short parables, Jesus speaks of using the gift of time faithfully:

Death comes to us like a ***"thief in the night,"*** Jesus tells his listeners; therefore, we must always be ready to meet the Lord and enter his "kingdom" with "belts tightened" and no worldly encumbrances to distract us or hinder our journey. The first generations of Christians read this parable as an indication that Christ would return in their lifetimes, in the middle of the great Paschal night. While we pay little or no attention to the reality of our own deaths and carry on as if we will live forever, the fact is that life is fragile and fleeting. If we have truly embraced the spirit of the Gospel, we are always conscious of the brevity of this life and live our days in joyful anticipation of the next.

Throughout the Gospels, Jesus again uses the image of a ***banquet*** to portray the coming reign of his Father. Luke includes the image in his Gospel, as well, with an interesting twist: Those who have embraced the spirit of servanthood taught by Jesus the Master will be served by the Master himself at his table in heaven. Jesus targets the parable to the leaders of the Jewish establishment who have used their positions to advance their own prestige and wealth at the expense of the people they were appointed to serve. While God casts out the exploiters from his kingdom, the faithful leader-servants will be served by the Messiah himself at God's great banquet.

The third parable (which concludes the Roman pericope for today) is Luke's version of Jesus' story of the ***watchful steward*** who faithfully conducts the responsibilities entrusted to him by his master. This life on earth is a time that has been entrusted to us by God and must be about the business of preparing for the life of the world to come. God has entrusted to each one of us gifts, talents and blessings not for our own good but to employ for the benefit of others, without counting the cost or demanding a return. The faithful disciple lovingly and selflessly uses whatever he or she possesses to bring God's reign of hope, justice and compassion to reality in this time and place of ours.

By the wisdom and grace of God, may we bridge that chasm between the treasures of God and the things we are accumulating; may the treasures of our own hearts mirror the treasures of God.

Father in heaven,
we thank you for the gift of time you have given us.
May we use these precious, limited moments
you have entrusted to us
wisely and creatively.
In every minute and day and week and month
  and year of our lives,
may we make ready the wedding feast of your Son,
welcoming and serving others
  at our own humble tables
as we await the great banquet of your kingdom.

Sunday 20 / Proper 15

"I have come to set the earth on fire, and how I wish it were already blazing …! Do you think that I have come to establish peace on earth? No, I tell you, but rather division."

Luke 12: 49–56

"You've got to be taught …"

It was Tommy's first day at a new school. Looking for his sixth-grade classroom, he asked directions from a boy walking by. The boy quietly pointed to Tom's room, not smiling, never looking directly at Tom. Before Tom could thank him, he disappeared.

At recess Tom caught up with the boy who had helped him. The boy said his name was Kyle and that he was in the sixth grade too. They talked about the stuff that sixth-graders talk about. At one point, Kyle almost smiled. They met after school, shot some baskets, and got some Cokes. Kyle asked about the iPod Tom had in his backpack; when Kyle put on the earbuds and listened to the music, it was the only genuine smile he showed. Tom watched in awe at Kyle's prowess on the court — Kyle seemed to be able to sink the ball perfectly from anywhere, at will. Kyle showed Tommy how to gauge his shots more accurately.

That evening, Tom's parents asked how the first day went. O.K., he said. He liked his teachers for the most part, lunch was all right, and he met this new kid. A look of concern immediately came over their faces when Tom mentioned Kyle's name. Maybe Tom better steer clear of Kyle, they suggested. There were stories about his family … his father never seemed to be around … there was an arrest or something — one of Kyle's brothers has a long record, they thought.… Didn't they live in the projects?

But what did that have to do with Kyle? Tom wondered. He's a good kid.

Still, Mom and Dad said, they'd feel more comfortable if Tom didn't spend too much time with Kyle.

The next day at school, Kyle was the first to see Tom. "Hi," Kyle said — still not exactly smiling, but with an easiness that wasn't there yesterday.

"Hey," Tom said.

And Tom kept walking.

Tom never spent any more time with Kyle.

And Tom never really told his parents anymore about school … or anything else that mattered.

Tommy has just discovered for the first time in his young life that Christ-like charity and justice can be at odds with the world of adults. He is learning that Gospel faith is not the safe, warm, reassuring blanket we believe it to be.

When Luke wrote the few lines that we read today, Christians were living through difficult circumstances. In many places they were treated with ridicule, disdain and intolerance. Jesus' words are addressed to them and to all Christians who have paid dearly for living their faith in their time and place.

Fire is a Scriptural symbol of judgment. The Lord will judge the hearts of all men and women in the light of his "blaze." The "fire" Jesus ignited on earth has burned in the hearts of many Christians ever since: They struggle on, despite ostracism and opposition, to live their baptisms. They carry on, their commitment inflamed by mercy, justice and compassion. They persevere, knowing that the promise of the resurrection is fulfilled only through the cross and the crucifixion of oppression, injustice and hatred.

The word used in the original text that reads here as baptism actually means a "plunging," a total submersion. Jesus continues on to Jerusalem where he will be "plunged" into the Passover of the new covenant into which, through baptism, we will all be "plunged," as well.

Today's Gospel pericope is not a comforting message. Families and households will be divided over the hard demands of the Gospel of reconciliation, justice and servanthood. In its call for personal conversion, Jesus' Gospel can be divisive and confrontational. Jesus' words challenge us to grow beyond our fears, our biases, our narrow-mindedness; he demands more courage, more compassion, more humility than we believe we are capable of. Despite the divisive consequences, Christ calls us to the hard work of seeking the mercy and justice of God and living his Gospel of reconciliation and peace in our own time and place, regardless of the cost.

To live the Gospel faithfully is to become a contradiction to those around us. The Gospel calls us to risk power, prestige and even acceptance to stand up for the equality, justice, compassion and reconciliation that every individual possesses by virtue of being a son and daughter of God.

Ask Tommy some time. He's learning — the hard way.

Christ our Redeemer,
make us signs of contradiction to our world:
may we be the fire of justice and righteousness,
may we be immersed in the waters
of humility and selflessness.
As we stand alone for the sake of what is right and just,
may we remember that you stand with us.
As we find ourselves isolated and ridiculed,
may we find meaning and hope in the example
of your own life.

Sunday 21

"Strive to enter through the narrow gate, for many, I tell you, will attempt to enter but will not be strong enough. After the master of the house has arisen and locked the door, then you will stand outside knocking and saying, 'Lord, open the door for us.' He will say to you in reply, 'I do not know where you are from.... ' For behold, some are last who will be first, and some are first who will be last."

Luke 13: 24–30
[Roman lectionary]

Passages

In the first year of life, the baby struggles to take his or her first steps. The child can charge around the room — as long as there is furniture, railings or Daddy's long legs to hold on to. But the child will never walk until he or she lets go and stands on his or her own.

First graders begin school excited about the great possibilities that await them: the books they will be able to read, the devices they will be able to use to count things, to measure things, to keep track of things. But first, they have to master the sounds of the 26 letters of the alphabet and the basic tables of numbers.

Later, in high school and college, will come the opportunities to learn the skills on which to build successful and satisfying careers — once the future writers, scientists and economists pass the basic "101" courses.

A man and woman meet. They get to know and like each other; they find that mysterious "specialness" in one another; their friendship blossoms into love. But only when one works up the courage to propose marriage will they take the first step together to "live happily ever after."

Life is a series of "narrow doors" through which we have to pass — and there is no easy way to pass through them. Like Jesus' journey to Jerusalem, our journey is difficult and painful; doubt, despair and ridicule are among the obstacles we must encounter. Jesus employs three images in today's Gospel that speak of the disciple's life journey:

The narrow door: The major cities of Palestine were built with walls surrounding the perimeter. At the entrance to the city was a gate with three entry ways: The center arch was tall and wide to accommodate camels and carts of goods and trains of baggage; on each side of this main arch were lower, narrower passage ways: individuals with no baggage could avoid the traffic and enter the city quickly. Throngs of people could enter the city only through the great doors at the city's entrance. Jesus, however, calls us to enter the city of God through the "narrow door" — through the lonely, humble entryway of the human heart.

The locked door: Conversion is not an instantaneous transformation in which we go from Godlessness to holiness. Our lives are a constant process of conversion, of working to become the people God has called us to become. Faith is not a pre-ordained condition nor an all-purpose "pass key" nor a guaranteed reservation to the hereafter. God demands of us a personal, committed response to his gift of faith as the key to the promise of the resurrection.

The feast: God's invitation to the banquet of heaven is extended to all men and women of good will, not just to those who presume themselves to be God's special elite. The kingdom of God does not belong to the powerful, the learned or the religious elite, but to the people of the Beatitudes — the poor in spirit, the just, the humble, the peacemaker.

To embrace the attitude of the "narrow door," Dorothy Day wrote, "is to bring about a revolution of heart.... When we begin to take the lowest place, to wash the feet of others, to love others with that burning love, that passion, which led to the Cross, then we can truly say, 'Now I have begun.' "

Lord God,
show us the way through the narrow door of humility
that we may live lives of integrity and purpose;
entrust to us the keys of justice and compassion
that unlock for us and for all the door to your reign;
welcome us to your table in heaven
as we welcome you, in the poor and forgotten,
to our tables.

Proper 16

Jesus cures a crippled woman on the Sabbath: " … ought not this woman, a daughter of Abraham whom Satan bound for eighteen long years, be set free from this bondage on the sabbath day?"

Luke 13: 10–17
[Common lectionary]

"The great teachings"

The story is told in Japan of a Zen priest who sought to have the great teachings printed in the Japanese language for all to read and study. He assembled the texts, translated them into Japanese, and then traveled the length and breadth of Japan to solicit funds for the project. Occasionally he would receive a gift as large as a hundred pieces of gold from a wealthy landowner or merchant; but mostly he received small coins from peasants. The priest expressed equal gratitude to each donor, regardless of the amount.

After ten long years of travel, the priest finally collected the funds necessary to begin the time-consuming work of printing the book. But just as the engravings were about to begin, a great flood destroyed the homes of thousands of people. The priest used the money he had collected for his cherished project to help the homeless and starving victims.

The priest then began again the long, hard task of raising the funds for his book of the great teachings. After many years of travel and begging, he had collected the money needed for the printing. But when the engraving was to start a second time, a great epidemic swept through the land. The priest gave away all the money he had collected to buy medicine for the sick and dying.

A third time the priest set out to raise the needed funds. Twenty years later, his dream of a book of the great teachings, written in Japanese, was finally realized.

The printing blocks that produced the edition are on display in a monastery in Kyoto. The Japanese tell their children that the old priest is actually responsible for three editions of the great teachings: the first two are invisible — and far superior to the third.

The curing of the crippled woman on the Sabbath is found only in Luke's Gospel (though Jesus performs similar miracles on the Sabbath in the other Gospels). In this account, Jesus defies the sensibilities of the synagogue leaders and cures a crippled woman on the Sabbath day. While the leaders of the synagogue are concerned with the regulations of the Sabbath observance, Jesus extends his compassion and mercy to the woman. Jesus' healing of the woman does not undermine the holiness of the Sabbath — on the contrary, Jesus' action irrevocably links the prayer and ritual of the Sabbath to the unlimited and unconditional mercy of God.

To be worthy of God, our own Sabbath observance must be centered in the very forgiveness and reconciling love of the God we praise. The prayers we speak and the faith we profess — whether sung in choir or engraved on printing blocks — find their meaning and purpose in the selfless giving and compassion they inspire us to take on.

Generosity is the most beautiful prayer we offer; compassion is the most effective Gospel we preach.

May compassion and justice be our prayer to you,
O God;
may our work to heal divisions
and our care for those in need
be the incense of our praise;
may our struggle to forgive and seek forgiveness
be the gift we offer to you
in gratitude for your blessings to us.
By our efforts to love and forgive,
however small and humble,
transform our days into an eternal Sabbath
of peace and joy for all humankind.

" ... every one who exalts himself will be humbled, but the one who humbles himself will be exalted.... when you hold a banquet, invite the poor, the crippled, the lame, the blind; blessed indeed will you be because of their inability to repay you."

Luke 14: 1, 7–14

Flesh and blood

In Erich Maria Remarque's brilliant and bitter story of the horrors of war, *All Quiet On the Western Front,* Paul Baumer, the 19-year-old German soldier who narrates the tale, huddles in a large hole made by an exploded shell. Suddenly, a French soldier jumps into the hole. Instinctively, Baumer stabs the intruder with a small dagger he has concealed. Baumer discovers that the man's name is Duval, that he is a husband and father, and he works as a printer. Soon the wounded Duval dies, propped up against Baumer.

In the silence that follows, the terrified Baumer "speaks" to the dead Duval:

"Comrade, I did not want to kill you. If you jumped in here again, I would not do it, if you would be sensible, too. But you were only an idea to me before, an abstraction that lived in my mind and called for its appropriate response. It was that abstraction that I stabbed. But now, for the first time, I see you are a man like me. I thought of your hand grenades, of your bayonet, of your rifle; now I see your life and your face and our fellowship.

"Forgive me, comrade. We always see it too late. Why do they never tell us that you are poor devils like us, that your mothers are just as anxious as ours, and that we have the same fear of death, and the same dying and the same agony — forgive me, comrade; how could you be my enemy?

"If we threw away these rifles and these uniforms you could be my brother.... Take twenty years of my life, comrade, and stand up — take more, for I do not know what I can even attempt to do with it now."

Throughout the Gospels, Jesus calls us to see one another not as abstract labels nor impersonal demographics but to welcome one another as real flesh and blood, sacred and holy as children of the God who is Father of us all. Such a perspective is grounded in humility.

Gospel humility (a key theme of Luke's Gospel) is not some form of religious sadomasochism motivated by self-hatred or obsequiousness. As taught by Jesus, humility is the awareness of who we are before God; of our constant need for God and our dependence on God for everything; of the limitlessness of God's love and forgiveness. The spirit of Gospel humility is the realization that we share with every human being the sacred dignity of being made in the image and likeness of God.

In today's Gospel, Jesus urges his own to embrace the attitude of seeking the "lowest places" for the sake of others, promising that at the banquet of heaven God will exalt such humility. In calling us to invite to our tables "those who cannot repay you," Jesus challenges us to imitate the love of God: doing what is right, good and just for the joy of doing so, not out of a sense of duty, self-interest or the need to feel superior or in control.

To be humble as Christ teaches humility is to see one another with the same vision that God sees us. The humility of the Gospel is to realize that all the blessings we have received come as a result of the depth of God's love and not because of anything we have done to deserve it. Confronted with this realization, all we can do is to try and return that love to those around us.

Such humility demands a new perspective, a new vision for seeing ourselves and one another. As a result of his tragic encounter with Duval, the young German soldier Baumer will never see life the same way again. He will never see men and women as mere labels or numbers or nationalities. He will never see himself as anyone's superior. Baumer has witnessed the fragileness of life and dignity that binds every human being that is the beginning of Christ-like humility.

May we embrace your Son's spirit of humility,
O God,
that we may realize the many blessings
you have given us.
Let our gratitude compel us to make places for all
at our tables,
welcoming them as our brothers and sisters
in Christ Jesus.

The parables of the tower and the king preparing for war: "Whoever does not carry his own cross and come after me cannot be my disciple … Anyone who does not renounce all his possessions cannot be my disciple."

Luke 14: 25–33

Cross walk

It may begin with a phone call in the middle of the night: a child has been in an accident, a parent has suddenly taken ill.

Or it may take the form of a lesson plan you struggle to lead your students through — kids who are far more interested in video games than subject/verb agreement, algebraic equations, or the Gospel of Luke.

It may be trying to maintain peace in the family despite a disagreeable relative or struggling to keep the project on schedule despite a clueless boss or an incompetent team member.

It can come as ridicule or addiction. It is often formed by the intersecting beams of despair and abandonment, of exhaustion and anger.

It may be the money you have — or the money you don't have. It may be the passion you have for a cause or the compassion you feel for the victims.

The cross — those struggles and challenges we can't avoid, those people and situations we try to sidestep, the hard reality that forces us to delay our hopes and abandon our dreams.

But the cross is not necessarily an instrument of torture or a death sentence. Borne on the right shoulders, the cross can be a means of healing, an instrument for transformation, a vehicle for resurrection. It begins with realizing that another shoulder bears that load with us:

Christ's.

Today's Gospel is Jesus' treatise on the nature and demands of discipleship (while similar words appear in the other synoptics, Luke expands on Jesus' words, including the images of the tower and the king preparing for war). Jesus' sobering words are meant to make us fully aware of the cost of discipleship before we embrace something we are not prepared for. Jesus calls us to seek reconciliation rather than dominance, to love and forgive without limit or condition, to give totally and completely regardless of the cost or sacrifice. Such is the cross Jesus asks us to take up.

Some translations of today's Gospel ascribe rather harsh words to Jesus: in some texts, Jesus speaks of "turning one's back" on family; in other translations, the verb "hate" is used. A more precise translation of the idiom here means that whoever prefers the love of family or self to Christ cannot be his follower. Often we refuse to "let go" of things that are making our lives so much less than we want them to be. The gifts of God can only be grasped with the open hands of humility and prayer; the grasping hands of materialism and self-centeredness condemn us to a life of emptiness.

The images of the unfinished tower and the king preparing to wage war illustrate the frustration and ultimate failure of the disciple who does not give himself/herself totally to the Gospel (Jesus may well have drawn both illustrations from the news of the day: King Herod had launched a number of major construction projects in Caesarea Maritima, Jericho and Jerusalem; there were also rumblings of war between Herod Antipas and King Aretas of Nabaea over Herod's planned divorce of Aretas' daughter). When a follower of Jesus begins to hold anything back in imitating Christ, discipleship becomes a charade. As the tower builder and the king making battle plans quickly realize, our days are limited — too limited to squander. Jesus challenges us to live every moment of our lives as a time for preparation and "planning" for much greater and lasting things than this world of ours offers.

The cross takes many forms in our lives; our road to Calvary is filled with unexpected turns, deep ruts and rocky obstacles. But we cannot be Jesus' disciples without taking up whatever cross is laid on our shoulders. But as disciples, we carry on with the certain hope that we do not carry our crosses alone; in faith, we know that every Good Friday is fulfilled with its Easter morning.

Christ Jesus,
give us the wisdom and grace to take up the crosses
laid upon our shoulders.
Help us to "crucify" our own narrow interests
and self-centered wants
so that we may bring to our families and communities
the joy and hope of your resurrection.

Sunday 24 / Proper 19

"Rejoice with me because I have found my lost sheep … because I have found the coin that I lost … because your brother was lost and has been found."

Luke 15: 1–32

"My shepherd is my D.R.E. …"

Every parish religious education director (D.R.E.) has had to deal with at least one family who seems perpetually lost: the parents who never read any of the materials sent home, who always seem to "lose" their child's class schedule, who are just too overwhelmed with work, school and sports schedules to make it to Mass on Sundays as a family. The D.R.E. spends as much time following up with visits and telephone calls to this one family as he or she does in organizing the entire program for the other families in the parish; the child's teacher devotes more time helping their unprepared child grasp that week's lesson than with the other children in the class.

The D.R.E. reaches a point where he or she wants to write them off and move on without them: *Why do they bother if it means so little to them? Why do I bother when they don't care*, the D.R.E. wonders, quite understandably.

But there are those moments when the "lost" are "found": when a child comes to understand — really understand — how much God loves that child and every child; when the First Eucharist celebration becomes a moment of conversion for the whole family; when parents come to appreciate what the D.R.E., the teachers and the parish have done for them. Dealing with "lost families" is frustrating, aggravating and, yes, unfair and unjust. But, through the grace of God, they are "found." It is an experience of great joy for the family — and for the D.R.E.

We all have "lost" sheep in our lives — well, if not lost, misplaced. They monopolize our attention, usurp our energy, and demand more of our time than they are reasonably entitled to. They anger us, frustrate us, and sometimes even turn on us. But Jesus asks us to "hang tough" with them, not to reject them or move on without them, because every one is precious and "worth it" in the eyes of God.

Today's Gospel is made up of three "parables of the lost" in chapter 15 of Luke's Gospel. Luke wrote his Gospel at a time when the Christian community was embroiled in the Church's first great controversy: Many Jewish Christians were indignant that Gentiles should be welcomed into the Church without first embracing the traditions and laws of Judaism.

In these three parables, we enter God's world: God communicates the depth of his love in his unconditional and complete forgiveness; his mercy breaks through and demolishes all human restrictions. The Pharisees could not imagine a God who actually sought out sinful men and women, a God who is more merciful in his judgments than we are, a God who never gives up hope for a sinner.

The three parables in today's pericope are unique to Luke's Gospel:

The parable of the lost sheep: Shepherding demanded toughness and courage — it was not a job for the weak and fearful. Responsible for every sheep in his charge, a shepherd was expected to fight off every threat from wild animals to armed poachers. Shepherds were often required to risk their lives to rescue a single lost sheep who wandered off in the dangerous wilderness terrain. Like the responsible shepherd, God does whatever is necessary to seek out and bring back to his loving providence every lost soul.

The parable of the lost coin: Finding a small silver coin in a dark, dusty, dirt-floored Judean house was nearly impossible, but so great was the value of any coin to the poor that a woman would turn her poor hovel inside out in search of such a treasure. So loved is every soul that God, too, goes to whatever lengths necessary to find and bring back the lost.

The parable of the prodigal son: This is probably the most inaccurately titled story in all of literature. Jesus' tale is really about the great love of the prodigal's father, who forgives his son and joyfully welcomes him home even before the son can bring himself to ask. The father's joy stands in sharp contrast to the prodigal's brother, who cannot even bring himself to call the prodigal his "brother" — in confronting his father, he angrily refers to the brother as "this son of yours." But the father is a model of joyful reconciliation that Jesus calls his disciples to seek in all relationships.

The most extraordinary element of all of Jesus' teachings is the revelation of a God who loves each and every one of us uniquely and individually, as a parent loves his/her most beloved child. God's love for us is eternally forgiving, constantly inviting, never limited or conditional; God throws away no one; God does not write off anyone as hopeless or irredeemable. In the three parables in today's Gospel, Christ challenges each one of us to the hard work of repairing broken relationships, of restoring community in the wake of division and dysfunction. Despite the difficulty we sometimes have in accepting the success or good things happening to others, the Gospel calls us to rejoice for and with those who conquer adversity, who struggle to rebuild their lives, who manage to rise from the depth of despair and death to fulfillment and hope.

Gracious God,
give us the patience to seek out and bring back
the lost, the forgotten, the rejected, the alienated
into our own families and communities.
Never let us forget that you always search us out
when we are lost.
May we possess a measure of that love
for those you send us out
to search for,
to seek out,
to wait up for and welcome back.

The parable of the dishonest steward: "The children of this world are more prudent in dealing with their own generation than are the children of light ... No servant can serve two masters. He will either hate one and love the other, or be devoted to one and despise the other. You cannot serve both God and mammon."

Luke 16: 1–13

Land grab

In a story by Leo Tolstoy, a young farmer named Pahom took over the family farm and made quite a success of it. Soon he bought the neighbor's farm, and then that neighbor's neighbor's farm, and so on until he owned thousands of acres of land. He continued to buy land until he was the largest landholder in the district.

But it was not enough. Pahom wanted more. A traveler told him of the far away country of the Bashkirs, where acres and acres of the most beautiful land were waiting to be cultivated. Pahom investigated the traveler's story and found that it was true. Pahom immediately sold his land and homestead at a hefty profit and journeyed to the land of the Bashkirs.

Upon his arrival, Pahon presented himself to the Bashkir chief. Pahom offered to buy as much land as they would sell. The chief said the price was set: One thousand rubles a day.

One thousand rubles a *day?* What kind of measure is that?

"We do not know how to reckon it out," said the chief. "We sell it by the day. As much as you can go round on your feet in a day is yours, and the price is one thousand rubles a day."

Pahom was shocked. "But in a day you can get round a large track of land."

"And it will be yours," the chief replied. "But there is one condition: If you don't return on the same day to the same spot where you started, your money is lost."

The excited Pahom paid the money and agreed to begin his trek the next morning. That night the excited Pahom could hardly sleep. The virgin soil was the most beautiful he had ever seen, rich and black, level and stoneless. All of it would be his.

Just before sunrise the next morning, Pahom met the chief and his council at the appointed place. As the sun appeared over the horizon at dawn, Pahom dug his spade into the dirt, marking his starting point. The race was on.

Pahom walked as fast as he could, making marks along the way. As the day grew warmer, he cast aside his coat. Soon he was running. By noon he was very pleased at the great distance he walked — but time was wasting. He did not stop to eat, but kept up his pace, almost running. Pahom would not even take time to rest or take a drink of water. Although near exhaustion, the promise of land kept him going.

All afternoon he ran.

As the sun began to set, Pahom realized that he had gone too far. He had less than an hour to make it back to the starting spot. Horrified at his blunder, Pahom ran faster and faster, his legs becoming heavier and heavier. The sun began to set over the western horizon. Pahom could see the chief and the Bashkir elders waiting for him. Pahom dragged his body across the plain, crying for more time.

With the sun disappearing, Pahom dropped to his knees before reaching the mark he had made at sunrise. But he had no strength left to make his final mark. Broken and exhausted, Pahom collapsed before the chief.

The Bashkirs picked up his shovel and buried Pahom on the spot. Six feet from his head to his heels was all he needed.

Throughout the Gospels, Jesus constantly warns his followers of the dangers of money and possessions. Too often, we let what we possess possess us. Today's Gospel repeats the warning — with a startling twist.

The parable of the shrewd business manager (found only in Luke's Gospel) is one of the most difficult parables of Jesus to grasp. Stewards collected rents and debts for their employers, charging interest on outstanding debts that would go to the steward. The steward in the parable is not trying to hide anything from his master — in fact, he wants the master to discover how he has altered the books. The steward's hope is that his shrewdness and cleverness will win back his employer's favor; if not, the steward will at least have made some grateful friends along the way.

At first reading, it appears that Jesus is condoning extortion. But Jesus admires not the manager's lack of scruples but his decisiveness and ingenuity in taking control of his situation. He commends the shrewd manager for his deftness in getting things done. As the steward goes to such great lengths to secure a place in this world, so should we seek to secure a place in the world to come.

Like the shrewd manager and his demanding master, we can become so obsessed with the pursuit of wealth and the manipulation of power ("dishonest wealth") that we seem to give up a piece of our humanity in the process. Christ calls us to something far greater: to use that same dedication of energy, ability and efficiency to make the reign of God a reality in our own time and place ("true wealth"). Christ warns his hearers not to trust in wealth for its own sake but to use wealth — whatever form our "wealth" takes — to establish the Father's kingdom of compassion, reconciliation and justice in our midst.

Jesus' parable challenges us to be as eager and as ingenious for the sake of God's reign, to be as ready and willing to use our time and money to accomplish great things in terms of the Gospel as we are to secure our own security and enjoyment. Jesus appeals to the "children of light" to be as enterprising and resourceful in pursuing the reign of God as this steward is in making a place of himself in this world. We must restore money as the means to an end and not as the end itself, for we are only stewards of our Master's property.

God of all good things,
give us the humility of spirit
to live lives centered in gratitude
  for all you have given us;
give us the generosity of heart
to open our hands to share your blessings
  with all your sons and daughters;
give us the wisdom and perspective
to use what you have given us
  to establish your reign of justice and peace
  in our own time and place.

Sunday 26 / Proper 21

"Lying at the rich man's door was a poor man named Lazarus, covered with sores, who would gladly have eaten his fill of the scraps that fell from the rich man's table."

Luke 16: 19–31

"To have enough"

Novelist Kurt Vonnegut told this story during a commencement address at Rice University:

Vonnegut was invited to a lavish party thrown by a multimillionaire on his estate on Long Island. At the party, Vonnegut ran into a friend, Joseph Heller, author of *Catch-22*.

"Joe," Vonnegut asked," how does it make you feel to realize that only yesterday our host probably made more money than *Catch-22* [one of the most popular books of all time] has grossed worldwide over the past 40 years?"

Heller said, "I have something he can never have."

"What's that, Joe?"

"The knowledge that I've got enough."

Vonnegut concluded his story to the graduates:

"[Heller's] example may be of comfort to many of you, who in later years will have to admit that something has gone terribly wrong — and that, despite the education you received, you have somehow failed to become billionaires. This can happen to people who are interested in something other than money, other than the bottom line. We call such people saints — or I do …"[6]

To possess such a sense of gratitude to God that we can accept the reality that we, indeed, have "enough" is a mark not only of the wise but of the faithful, and, yes, in the words of Kurt Vonnegut, the "saint." God has entrusted each one of us with many gifts, talents and blessings.

They have not been given to us so that we can accrue more for ourselves but have been entrusted to us in order to use them selflessly and lovingly for the benefit of others, without counting the cost or setting conditions or demanding a return.

The rich man (sometimes known as "Dives") in today's Gospel fails to grasp that sense of responsibility for his blessings. He is not really a bad man, but a self-centered, complacent one. Dives' sin is his remaining oblivious to the plight of Lazarus (a name which means "God's help") at his gate and his ready acceptance of the poverty of so many and wealth in the hands of so few like himself as the natural, inevitable order of things. It was not his wealth that kept him from "Abraham's bosom," but his faithless stewardship of what he had. Given so much, Dives could do a great deal for the poor around him — yet he is too uncaring and oblivious even to see the plight of one poor beggar at his gates.

May we have the wisdom to realize that we have "enough" and the grace to understand the responsibility for the blessings God has entrusted to us.

O God,
open our eyes to see the poor, the needy, the forgotten
  at our own gates
and open our hearts to welcome them
into our lives with compassion and respect.
In welcoming the Lazaruses to our tables,
may we welcome you;
in giving to them,
may we give you thanks for the privilege
of being able to give and share what you, in your
  goodness,
have entrusted to us.

"If you have faith the size of a mustard seed, you would say to this mulberry tree, 'Be uprooted and planted in the sea,' and it would obey you.... When you have done all you have been commanded, say 'We are unprofitable servants; we have done what we were obliged to do.'"

Luke 17: 5–10

One less rocket scientist

The college's admissions committee was reviewing applications from high school seniors for the new freshmen class. They plowed through hundreds of student essays on why the writer should be admitted to the school; their eyes glazed over as they read essay after essay on the promise and potential of all of these future presidents, rocket scientists, doctors and lawyers.

But one applicant's essay caught the committee's attention for its surprising lack of pretense. The student's essay read in part:

"I am not a great student nor am I a leader. You could say that I am incredibly average. I work very hard for the grades I get.... For the past three summers, I have worked at a camp for children with cancer. At first, I was terrified that I would say something stupid or I would do something that would add to their pain. I was surprised at how much I enjoyed working with these kids. I have been even more surprised at everything I have learned from them about life and death, about coping with illness and disappointment, about what is really important and good.

"I would like to work with chronically ill and physically challenged children. I would like to pursue a degree in education and psychology so that I might try to give these boys and girls something of what they have given me."

The student's application was immediately put in the *Admit* pile. The committee felt that they had enough presidents and Nobel laureates to choose from; they wanted to make sure they had room for one good, dedicated teacher.

Perseverance and humility — what the admissions committee sees in this student's essay Jesus exalts in the two images in today's Gospel:

The gift of faith is like the mustard seed, among the tiniest of seeds. The seed of faith needs to be nurtured or else it withers and dies; but allowed to grow, it yields the greatest of harvests. The mustard seeds that each one of us plants will yield not only the greatest harvest but also the most enduring and rooted harvest. It requires trust in the potential of the seed and perseverance in nurturing the seed to realize that potential. With "mustard seed" faith, we can bring the presence of God into the most ordinary dimensions of our lives and the lives of those we love.

In the light of real faith, we realize our total dependence on the providence of God. To God's graciousness we owe everything, beginning with the first breath we take. We recognize ourselves as his "useless servants," deserving nothing by our own account. Faith begins with the gratitude and humility of the servant in today's Gospel: to understand that the gift of faith requires justice, compassion and forgiveness; to realize, in the light of God's love, how blessed we have been and to see ourselves and others as brother and sister "servants" at the table of the Father. The only adequate response we can make to God's unfathomable and immeasurable goodness is to live lives of joyful gratitude and humble servanthood.

Instill in us, O Lord, the spirit of mustard seed faith:
despite our qualms and fears,
make us vehicles of your compassion
for the sake of others;
despite our self-consciousness and hesitation,
make us planters of your peace, justice
and reconciliation
in our own small corner of the Father's kingdom.

Sunday 28 / Proper 23

One of the lepers, realizing that he had been healed, returned, glorifying God in a loud voice; and he fell at the feet of Jesus and thanked him. He was a Samaritan. Jesus said in reply, "Ten were cleansed, were they not? Where are the other nine?"

Luke 17: 11–19

The nine other stories

So where *were* the other nine lepers who had been healed?

One of the now-clean lepers went off to build a new life for himself. He busied himself seeking work, a new place to live, putting down roots for himself, and, maybe he hoped, a family. He became so busy building a new life that he forgot the great blessing that was his.

But another one of the lepers was immediately overwhelmed with fear and worry: *What do I do now? I can't beg anymore. I have to find work. But I have no skills; I've never learned how to do anything. Who will hire me? How will I eat?* So worried and fearful was the once unclean leper for his future that he was paralyzed from doing anything. So he remained huddled at the gate, afraid and alone, like a leper.

Still another leper, realizing that he was now clean, determined to even the score with everyone who ever laughed at him, scorned him, ignored him, inflicted so many cruelties and indignities on him because of his illness. *They will pay for what they did to me,* he vowed. Obsessed with vengeance, he never, for a moment, experienced any joy in his cure.

One of the lepers, finally freed from his sufferings, ran as far away from the place as he could. All he wanted to do was forget his old life — and everyone and everything about it. He made himself deaf to the cries of the suffering of others — but could never run away far enough not to hear them.

And, of course, there was one leper who went out and celebrated — and celebrated and celebrated. His newfound joy lasted as long as the wine did. Once the wine disappeared, so did the camaraderie. He had to face his new life completely lost and alone.

There was one leper who didn't believe he was made clean. Why would anyone — least of all God — want to do this for him? There had to be a catch. So he did nothing; he just waited and waited for his leprosy to return. In his own mind, he was never healed.

And so the nine lepers went their separate ways. But without a sense of gratitude for the miracle they had experienced, the miracle didn't last very long. For their fears, their angers, their repressions, their skepticisms, their misplaced hopes and values just made them lepers all over again.

The grateful Samaritan leper is another of the great saints of Luke's Gospel. Terrified communities would cast out lepers from their midst, leaving them to fend for themselves outside the gates of their cities. This group of lepers included both Jews (Galileans) and Samaritans — they are so desperate in their plight that the usual bitter animosity between Jew and Samaritan evaporates between them. In their need, they have come to depend on one another.

Note that instead of curing them outright, Jesus sends the ten off to the priests who can legally verify a cure, putting the lepers' faith to the test. Only one — one of those despised Samaritans — realizes not only that he has been made clean but that he has been touched by God. His return to Jesus to give thanks reflects the healing that has taken place within the leper's soul as well as to his body. Faith is the recognition of the great love and compassion of God, a recognition that moves us to praise and acts of thanksgiving.

God is in our midst — and, like the nine lepers, we don't realize it. We never know that moment of realization experienced by the grateful leper: that God is present in our everyday lives, offering healing and hope. Our self-centeredness isolates us from one another; we find ourselves trapped by fear, distrust and hopelessness. But if we approach life with a sense of faith, we will come to realize the love of God in our midst — in the birth of our child, in the tenderness of our spouse, in the ability we have to bring joy and hope into the life of another.

For no other reason than love so deep we cannot begin to fathom it, God has breathed his life into us. The only fitting response we can make is to stand humbly before God in quiet, humble thanks. Such a constant sense of gratitude can transform cynicism and despair into optimism and hope and make whatever good we do experiences of grace.

Gracious God,
in you we are made whole;
we are created in your love,
sustained by your forgiveness,
transformed by your grace.
Make us a people of gratitude:
may we never forget that we have been given life
not because of anything we have done
  to warrant such a blessing
but because of your complete, unlimited
  and unconditional love.
May we realize that we have been cured
  despite the "illnesses" we face,
that our blessings far outweigh our struggles,
that we have reason to rejoice and hope
despite the sadness and anxieties we must cope with.

"There was a judge in a certain town who neither feared God nor respected any human being. And a widow in that town used to come to him and say, 'Render a just decision for me against my adversary.'"

Luke 18: 1–8

The persistent widow in our midst

It may be a spouse's Parkinson's disease, a parent's Alzheimer's, a sister's breast cancer, a child's leukemia. The illness of a loved one, a catastrophe striking their family, the suffering of someone dear to them transforms these mothers and fathers and sons and daughters and friends into dedicated advocates and determined guardians. They battle hospitals and insurance companies for the critical medical care needed by their loved one. They take on the most obstinate bureaucracies for the assistance and services their child is entitled to but denied. They work tirelessly to raise awareness, raise money, and, when necessary, raise Cain, so that their loved one may live as fully a life as possible, so that a cure might be found, so that other families will not have to experience the pain and anguish they have known.

These dedicated men and women are the Gospel widow in our midst. They face down the "dishonest judges" of arrogance and avarice; they take on the "fearful judges" of insensitivity and unawareness; they challenge the "judges who fear neither God nor respect any human being," save themselves.

Their love for the sick and suffering enables them to carry on "day and night"; their faith and conviction in the rightness of their cause empower them to carry on despite the frustration and inaction they face.

The very compassion of God is their hope and assurance that their prayer will be heard.

The focus of today's Gospel parable is not the evil judge but the persistent widow. The judge depicted here is not one of the Jewish elders but a paid magistrate appointed by the Roman governors. These magistrates were notoriously corrupt, extorting money from plaintiffs to secure favorable verdicts. The widow, typically defenseless in such dealings, persists until the judge just wants to be rid of her.

Jesus does not liken God to the unfeeling, insensitive judge but contrasts God to him: If such persistence will finally move such an unfeeling and corrupt figure as this judge, will not the God of mercy and love be moved by the cries of his own beloved people? The parable of the widow and the unjust judge (another parable found only in Luke's Gospel) calls us to perseverance in prayer — prayer that seeks not to force God's hand but prayer that opens our hearts and minds to his always available grace. As the great Jewish theologian Rabbi Abraham Joshua Heschel said, "to pray is to bring God back into the world … to expand his presence." Prayer does not seek to move God's heart for what we want; prayer is the opening up of our own heart and spirit to what God wants for us.

The persistent widow of today's Gospel lives among us: She is the poor, the struggling, the ignored, the forgotten, the victim of injustice whose sense of her own dignity enables her to fight on. Christ promises that the Father hears the worthy prayer of the Gospel widow in her many guises and that her perseverance in faith will one day be rewarded — and Jesus confronts us with our own culpability for the widow's plight when we become, in our obliviousness and self-absorption, "judges who neither fear God nor respect any human being."

Father of compassion,
may we pray not for what we seek but for what you seek;
may we discern not our wants but your will.
Open our hearts to hear your Word
  of justice and compassion;
open our hands that we may live that Word
in acts of generosity, consolation and forgiveness.

"The tax collector stood off at a distance and would not even raise his eyes to heaven but beat his breast and prayed, 'O God, be merciful to me a sinner.'"

Luke 18: 9–14

Worshipping ourselves at the altar

A writer had a dream in which she visited Hell. To her surprise, there was no fire or horrific scenes of torture and suffering. She was led along a labyrinth of dark, dank passages from which there were many doors leading to a number of cells. It was not like the Hell she had pictured at all. In fact, it seemed rather religious and "churchy." Each cell was identical. The central piece of furniture in each cell was an altar, and before each altar knelt sickly, weak, greeny-gray, ghostly figures in prayer and adoration.

"But whom are they worshipping?" the writer asked her guide.

"Themselves," was the reply. "This is pure self-worship. They are feeding on themselves and their own spiritual vitality in a kind of auto-spiritual-cannibalism. This is why they look so sickly and emaciated."

The writer was appalled and saddened by row upon row of cells with their non-communicating inmates, spending eternity in solitary confinement, themselves first, last and the only object of worship.[7]

In today's Gospel, the Pharisee and the tax collector (or "publican" as he is called in some translations) are caricatures of two extreme religious attitudes.

Pharisees were the "separated ones" who positioned themselves in society as the great keepers of the holy law. They were held in great esteem by the Jewish masses, despite the Pharisees' haughty condemnation of those they viewed as less than faithful.

Tax collectors were Jews who worked for Rome. To become a tax collector, one would bid for a certain territory by paying a sum that the government determined that area should yield in taxes. The tax collector then won the right to collect taxes from the people in that locale in order to recoup his investment and make a profit; as part of the arrangement, tax collectors could count on Roman cooperation to enforce their outrageous charges. It was a system that was rife with extortion, with little accountability demanded of the tax collectors and no avenues of recourse for the poor they preyed upon. Tax collectors were despised by Jewish society as thieves and collaborators.

The parable contrasts two very different attitudes of prayer. The Pharisee approaches God seeking the reward he feels he deserves. His prayer is really a testimonial to himself for all the good things the Pharisee has done to merit God's grace. The tax collector, on the other hand, realizes his nothingness before God. He comes before God seeking his mercy because of the good things God has done for undeserving sinners like himself. It is the prayer of the humble who come before God with an attitude of simple, heart-felt thanks for God's unconditional and limitless mercy that is heard and "exalted" before God.

Like the Pharisee, we can "use" God to justify our own self-centered belief systems and to advance our own idea of what the world should be. The Gospel of Jesus challenges us to embrace the humble, God-centered faith of the tax collector in today's Gospel. We live our faith and love for the God of graciousness not through the self-righteous piety of the Pharisee but through the humility of the tax collector, a humility that compels us to realize not only our littleness before God but also before one another.

O God, every moment we live is your gift to us.
Help us to remember that your very breath
gives life to us,
that your Spirit enables us to move and love and be.
Fill our hearts with gratitude —
gratitude that does not humiliate or depress us
but gratitude that fills us with joy

and the desire to share that joy with one another.
Draw us beyond our own sense of self
to realize that your Spirit of love is the center
  of our existence
and that it is only in imitating your Spirit
  of compassion and peace
that we find meaning and happiness in our lives.

Sunday 31 / Proper 26

Jesus looked up and said, "Zacchaeus, come down quickly, for today I must stay at your house." And he came down quickly and received him with joy. "Today salvation has come to this house ..."

Luke 19: 1–10

Salvation comes to *this* house ...

Teenage Daughter had been in a foul mood for what has seemed like an eternity. When her wise and patient mother had had enough of the sulking and rudeness, she sent the rest of the family off to the movies. Loading up with her daughter's favorite ice cream, Mom called her into the kitchen and asked her to have a seat. Mom scooped two big bowls. Nothing was said for a long time. But by the second scoops, the teenager began to open up. Mother and daughter talked the afternoon away. Because of a mother's patience, love, and a couple of pints of Ben & Jerry's ... *salvation comes to this house.*

It was a hard sell, but everyone (to Mom and Dad's surprise) bought into the idea. When their kids were older, they began a new family tradition. On a child's birthday, he or she would choose a charity, and the family would use the money that would have been used for gifts to make a donation in the child's name to that organization. The honoree would keep the decision secret until the birthday dinner; then, before blowing out the candles on the cake, the guest of honor would announce what charity would receive the gift and why. The tradition required some homework on the part of the birthday boy or girl (or parent), but everyone looked forward to being able to support a cause important to them. Loving parents instill in their children a sense of gratitude and a spirit of generosity ... *and salvation comes to this house.*

Every family has experienced some kind of short-term disaster: an unexpected illness, a sudden job loss, an unplanned-for budget-crippling expense. So when it happened to this family, Mom and Dad gathered everyone together, explained what had happened and why, and what every one — from the oldest to the youngest — could do to help get the family through the situation. And got through it they did — and along the way they became a closer, more understanding and loving family. With selfless love and patient understanding, a family can make it through hard times together … *and salvation comes to this house.*

In a scene that stunned those who witnessed it, salvation comes to the house of the little man in the sycamore tree. As the chief tax collector of Jericho, a very prosperous trade and agricultural village just northwest of Jerusalem, Zacchaeus was a very unpopular man with his fellow Jews (see last Sunday's notes on tax collectors). Though very wealthy, Zacchaeus (the name, ironically, means "clean") was a very unhappy and lonely man, deeply resented and feared by his neighbors because of his profession. Zacchaeus the outcast desperately seeks the peace of God taught by this rabbi Jesus — but it is Jesus who takes the initiative and calls out to Zacchaeus to climb down from the tree the short tax collector has climbed in order to get a glimpse of Jesus; Jesus then invites himself to Zacchaeus' house. In seeking out Zacchaeus, Jesus calls forth the good will of Zacchaeus that his neighbors fail to see.

The Messiah has come explicitly for the Zacchaeuses of the world: to lift up the fallen, to seek out the lost, to give hope to the poor and the forgotten. In our own humble efforts at kindness and understanding and our seemingly inconsequential acts of generosity and forgiveness we can bring to our own homes the salvation that Jesus brings to the house of the faithful Zacchaeus in today's Gospel.

Come, Lord Jesus, into our homes and hearts.
Help us to make the four walls of our own homes
places of peace and safety,
harbors of forgiveness and joy for one another,
houses where your salvation has come.

Sunday 32 / Proper 27

"They are the children of God because they are the ones who will rise … [The Lord] is not God of the dead but of the living, for to him all are alive."

Luke 20: 27–38

The Minister's Black Veil

In a tale by Nathaniel Hawthorne, the congregation of a small New England church is stunned one Sunday morning when their respected young minister, the Reverend Mr. Hooper, enters the church wearing a veil of black crepe over his face. The veil had a chilling effect on the congregation. The minister conducted the service as usual, making no reference to the veil — but its very presence evoked much fear, anxiety, mistrust and wild speculation among parishioners.

A deputation confronted the Reverend Mr. Hooper about the veil and his reasons for continuing to wear it. The minister answered simply, "If I hide my face for sorrow, there is cause enough, and if I cover it for secret sin, what mortal might not do the same?"

And for the rest of his long life, "Father" Hooper refused to take off the veil. His congregation eventually came to accept the veil and, over the years, their esteem for him and respect for his ministry grew. But even on his deathbed, when an attending minister tried to remove it, the elderly minister, though sick and confused, continued to clutch the veil tightly to his face.

"Why do you tremble for me alone?" he cried. "Tremble also at each other! Have men avoided me, and women shown me no pity, and children screamed and fled, only for my black veil?

"Look around me, and lo! on every visage do I see a Black Veil!"

Today's Gospel challenges us to see through the veils we hide behind — the veils of fear, mistrust, prejudice and ignorance that prevent us from living life in the complete joy of God.

After the Pharisees' several failed attempts to discredit Jesus, the Sadducees (a faction of priests and Jewish establishment types) challenge him. Unlike the Pharisees (the "separated ones" with whom they were often at odds), the Sadducees dismissed the oral tradition and any doctrinal developments not specifically ordered in the Pentateuch. They put no credence in the thousands of detailed regulations and rituals that the Pharisees embraced. The conservative Sadducees rejected the notion of angels or spirits, the belief in an afterlife and the idea of a Messiah.

The hypothetical case that the Sadducees concoct, based on Moses' teaching on marriage, is designed to ridicule the so-called "Messiah's" ludicrous teaching on the resurrection. Jesus, first, dismisses their attempt to understand the reign of God in human, worldly terms: the life of God transcends our understanding of human relationships and values. Citing the Sadducees' own cherished Mosaic writings, Jesus reminds them that God spoke to Moses of Abraham, Isaac and Jacob in the present tense, as still being alive before him and not as long-dead memories. God is not the God of the dead but the God of the living; Christ comes with the promise of always living in God and with God.

The legalistic and literal Sadducees cannot grasp the concept of a God who does not condemn evil and punish sinners; they cannot conceive of the God that Jesus reveals: a God of love that redeems and transforms.

We are often guilty of the Sadducees' limited vision of God: We struggle to gauge God by our standards, to measure God by our yardsticks, to define God by our systems of reasoning and understanding. But the God revealed by Jesus defies our explanations and designs. Our response to Jesus' call to be his disciples begins with opening our minds and spirits to become what God intends us to be.

Resurrection is the promise and hope of our faith as Christians — but resurrection is also an attitude, a perspective for approaching the decisions and complexities of our lives. In dying to our own worst impulses, disappointments, and the sometimes-overwhelming sense of hopelessness, we can rise to the heights of the life and love of God.

The Reverend Mr. Hooper exists to some extent in every one of us. We cover and surround ourselves with "black veils" of doubt, apprehension, rationalization; but the Easter Christ comes to remove those "veils" once and for all; he calls us forth from the tombs in which we wall ourselves off from others. Our faith in the Easter promise shatters any pretense or rationalization to don those "veils" again; in raising his Son from the dead, God raises us up as well, no longer "dead" in despair and cynicism but alive in the hope and joy of God's love.

God of the living,
may we live our lives in your love and compassion.
God of the resurrection,
may we bring your reconciliation and mercy
into tombs of despair and cynicism.
God beyond time,
bring us to the eternity of your reign.

"The days will come when there will not be left a stone upon another stone that will not be thrown down ... When you hear of wars and insurrections, do not be terrified; for such things must happen first, but it will not immediately end ... By your perseverance you will secure your lives."

Luke 21: 5–19

Today is "one of these days"

The widower opened the bottom drawer of his late wife's bureau and lifted out a tissue-wrapped package. He unfolded the tissue and handed his wife's sister a beautiful slip. The expensive garment was exquisite, handmade of silk and trimmed with intricate lace. The price tag was still attached.

"Jan bought this the first time we went to New York, at least eight or nine years ago. She never wore it. She was saving it for a special occasion. Well, I guess this is the occasion."

He took the slip and put it on the bed with the other clothes that they would bring to the funeral home. His hands lingered on the soft material for a moment, then he slammed the drawer shut. "Don't ever save anything for a special occasion," he said softly to his sister-in-law. "Every day you're alive is a special occasion."

The sister remembered those words through the funeral and the difficult days that followed as she helped her brother-in-law and niece attend to the sad chores that follow an unexpected death. She thought about the things her sister hadn't seen or heard or done, about all her late sister had done without realizing they were special. The words of her brother-in-law began to have a dramatic impact on her life. She remembers:

"I'm reading more and dusting less. I'm sitting on the deck and admiring the view without fussing about the weeds in the garden, I'm spending more time with my family and friends and less time in committee meetings.... I'm not 'saving' anything; we use our good china and crystal for every special event such as losing a pound, getting the sink unstopped, the first camellia blossom. I wear my good blazer to the market. 'Someday' and 'one of these days' are losing their grip on my vocabulary.... "I'm trying very hard not to put off, hold back, or save anything that would add laughter and luster to our lives. And every moment I open my eyes, I tell myself that it is special. Every day, every minute, every breath is ... a gift of God."[8]

Today's Gospel confronts us with the lessons this woman and her family learned in the unexpected death of her sister: that the time we are given in this life is precious, that God gives us this gift of life to embrace and be embraced by the love that is uniquely of God.

In today's reading, Jesus predicts the destruction of the temple and a chronicle of catastrophes — which is exactly what happened in the year 70 A.D., when more than a million Jews were killed in a desperate siege of Jerusalem by the Romans. Many Jews believed that the end of the world would be signaled by the destruction of the great temple at Jerusalem. It is against this background of this event that Luke writes his life of Jesus.

But Jesus does not teach dread here but hope. Trying to calculate the end of time is a waste of time; the signs of the apocalypse — war, plague, earthquakes — will appear in every age and there always will be self-proclaimed "messiahs" who will manipulate such events for their own power.

Jesus calls us not to be obsessed with the "stones" that will one day collapse and become dust but to seek instead the lasting things of the soul, the things of God. The temple may fall, but God remains. Jesus assures his followers that those who remain faithful to the vocation of discipleship will have nothing to fear when the end comes.

God beyond all measure,
be the light of hope that continues to burn brightly
when the temples we build collapse,
when the storms we encounter on our voyage sink us,
when disaster topples our sureties.
Help us to embrace your love that never ends,
your compassion that never fades,
your forgiveness that never falters.

Christ the King / Reign of Christ [Proper 29]

Above him there was an inscription: "This is the King of the Jews." The other criminal said, "Jesus, remember me when you come into your kingdom." Jesus replied to him, "Amen, I say to you, today you will be with me in paradise."

Luke 23: 35–43

The coming of the kingdom

Today we celebrate the reign of Christ in the least regal of places: the gallows.

In Luke's account of Jesus' crucifixion, Jesus struggles between life and death. He is jeered by the Jewish rulers who have engineered his death; he is taunted by the soldiers who have carried out his execution; even one of the two criminals hanging with him joins in his humiliation.

But the other criminal will have none of it. He realizes the injustice of Jesus' execution and senses God both with and within this rabbi hanging next to him. He rebukes the other criminal, admitting that both he and the other criminal are guilty, but that Jesus is innocent. And then, in a plea that has resounded through the centuries, he turns to Jesus and asks, "Jesus, remember me when you come into your kingdom."

The compassion and mercy that have marked his teachings and healings never leave Jesus. Among the last words the crucified Jesus speaks in Luke's Gospel is this promise: "Today you will be with me in Paradise."

On the gallows outside Jerusalem, the kingdom of God is founded. On a tree, the eternal reign of God's Christ begins.

On this last Sunday of the liturgical year, we stand on the edge of Paradise; we look through the doorway of heaven. In his promise to the "good thief," Jesus opens the door to true freedom; he invites us to embrace Paradise here and now; he has established the reign of God in our time and place. All we have to do — and it is no small thing — is to realize our need to be re-created by the love of God. The good thief realizes that need in himself and calls out to Jesus — and Jesus, in the last, painful moments of his own life, responds with compassion and hope. In the shadow of the cross, we are able to finally admit our need for healing, for peace, for God. In acknowledging our own need to forgive and be forgiven, to love and be loved, to give and be ministered to, Christ's promise of Paradise is ours.

But God's kingdom is not governed by the values and philosophies of this world; its progress is not measured in political and economic victories. The kingdom of God is the victory of the poor, the lost, the forgotten, the marginalized. The reign of Christ is the triumph of forgiveness, generosity, justice and peace. It is in this final moment of Jesus, his final act of compassion and forgiveness, that we realize God's kingdom has come.

Today's last Sunday of the liturgical year focuses on the kingdom of God Jesus has proclaimed in the Gospel readings of the past year: a kingdom that knows neither boundaries nor barriers, neither castes nor classes; a rule that is centered in service not tribute; a power that finds its authority in compassion; a court that seeks justice for the poor, the forgotten, the lost, the despairing; a culture and society that values forgiveness and reconciliation above any coin.

In baptism, we take on the work of establishing God's rule of justice, love, compassion and peace in our midst; we struggle to make Jesus' promise of Paradise a reality here and now. Inspired by the humility of Christ the Messiah-King, may we embrace the spirit of justice, integrity and humility of his cross and proclaim the truth revealed in the Gospel event: the uncompromising love of God for all men and women; the moral authority of humble servanthood to all who are our brothers and sisters in him; the never-failing hope of Easter resurrection over Calvary's cross.

Christ of compassion, Lord of reconciliation,
you have entrusted to us the work
of completing your kingdom.
May our embracing your spirit of selflessness,
may our imitating your compassionate servanthood,
reveal your presence in our midst
and establish Paradise in this time and place
as we journey throughout our lives
to the kingdom of your Father.

Notes

Advent

1. *The New York Times*, January 5, 1994.

Christmas

1. Adapted from *Leaping: Revelations and Epiphanies* by Brian Doyle (Chicago: Loyola Press, 2003), pages 154–155.

Lent

1. From *My Grandfather's Blessings* by Rachel Naomi Remen, M.D. (New York: Riverhead Books, 2000), pages 193–196.

Easter Triduum

1. From "Career ministry" by Garrett Keizer, *The Christian Century,* April 24–May 1, 2002.

Easter

1. From "Secret of Nyamirambo" by L. Gregory Jones, *The Christian Century*, December 13, 2005.
2. *Stone Soup* by Jan Eliot, March 27, 2004.
3. From "Parking lot palms" by Stephen Paul Bouman, *The Christian Century*, October 4, 2003.

Ordinary Time

1. *Overcoming Life's Disappointments* by Harold S. Kushner (New York: Alfred A. Knopf, 2006), page 74.
2. *My Grandfather's Blessings* by Rachel Naomi Remen, M.D. (New York: Riverhead Books), pages 203–204.
3. From *Praying at the Burger King* by Richard J. Mouw (Grand Rapids, Michigan: William B. Eerdmans Publishing Company, 2007), pages 84, 85.
4. From "Expect a call" by Kyle Childress, *The Christian Century*, January 9, 2007.
5. From "The Impossible Search" by Daniel Carey, Guideposts, May 1998.
6. *The Chronicle of Higher Education*, June 5, 1998.
7. Adapted from *Who Walk Alone* by Margaret Evening (London: Hodder and Stoughton, 1974), pages 38-39.
8. Author unknown, cited in *Spirituality and Health*, Summer 2000.